CREATIVE NONFICTION™

18

Intimate Details

CREATIVE NONFICTION™ 18

Editor
Lee Gutkind

Managing Editor
Leslie Boltax Aizenman

Business Manager
Patricia Park

Associate Editor
Tracy Ekstrand

Assistant Editor
Leslie Anne Mcilroy

Copy Editor
Susan Messer

Online Editor
Jonathan Cook

Production Manager
Kate W. Radkoff

Interns
Kate Luce Angell
Jessica Mesman

Editorial Board
Laurie Graham
Patricia Park
Lea Simonds

Editorial Advisory Board
Diane Ackerman
Annie Dillard
Tracy Kidder
Gay Talese

The Creative Nonfiction Foundation gratefully acknowledges the support of the Juliet Lea Hillman Simonds Foundation, Inc., the Pennsylvania Council on the Arts and Susan Ritz.

Address correspondence, unsolicited material, subscription orders and other queries to the Creative Nonfiction Foundation, 5501 Walnut St., Suite 202, Pittsburgh, PA 15232. Telephone: 412-688-0304; Fax: 412-683-9173; e-mail: info@creativenonfiction.org; Internet: http://www.creativenonfiction.org. Manuscripts will not be returned unless accompanied by a self-addressed, stamped envelope.

Creative Nonfiction (ISSN #1070-0714) is distributed in the U.S. by Ingram Periodicals Inc., 1240 Heil Quaker Blvd., La Vergne, TN 37068-7000, 800-627-6247; B. DeBoer, Inc., 113 East Center Street, Nutley, NJ 07110, 201-667-9300; Media Solutions, 9632 Madison Blvd., Madison, AL 35758, 615-213-0081. Creative Nonfiction is indexed in the American Humanities Index (Whitston Publishing Company).

Contents

LEE GUTKIND • *From the Editor* • 1

RUTHANN ROBSON • *Notes on My Dying* • 8

SUSAN MESSER • *Dots on the Page* • 18

MEREDITH HALL • *Killing Chickens* • 32

MELISSA BLOCH • *Second Chances* • 37

JENNIFER JEANNE PATTERSON • *White Girl in Harlem* • 61

HAL HERRING • *Silver Redhorse* • 73

SAMUEL PICKERING • *Familiar Things* • 83

RUSSELL TOMLIN • *Two Years* • 93

SARAH MASSEY-WARREN • *Bridges* • 109

AINE GREANEY • *Father* • 129

PHILIP GERARD • *Adventures in Celestial Navigation* • 138

BETWEEN THE LINES • *Report From a College Classroom* • 154
The Princeton Anthology of Writing

ISBN 1-928645-06-2

9 781928 645061 >

From the Editor
Beyond 9/11
Lee Gutkind

I was returning to Pittsburgh through New York's LaGuardia Airport—my first visit since the September 11 terrorist attacks. The security guard, a short, slender Latino in his late 20s, quickly rifled through my clothes and papers, but it was my shaving kit that attracted most of his attention. I had arrived an hour and a half before my scheduled flight, hoping to go standby on an earlier flight leaving in 25 minutes. So I was conscious of the seconds ticking away.

This man was intense and meticulous. He opened the top of my water-resistant, metallic blue Mini Mag-Lite and examined the batteries. A half-dozen years before in Washington, D.C., I had been trapped in a hotel on the 14th floor during a 26-hour blackout and almost killed myself in the pitch black trying to pack my belongings and subsequently locate the stairs and the emergency exit. Now I carry a flashlight wherever I travel.

But the guard found a second flashlight, a white plastic rectangular miniature from the Western Pennsylvania Cardiovascular Institute—a place I'd never heard of. The batteries were corroded and had leaked onto the case, so I threw it away.

He also discovered two nail clippers with miniature nail files about an inch long with moderately sharp points. If I intended to keep the nail files, he would have to check my shaving kit, tag it and send it separately as baggage, he said. I suggested he break them off from the clippers and discard them. We also trashed the cuticle scissors I use to trim my mustache.

Next he unscrewed the top from my After Bite Itch Eraser, housed in a plastic tube the size of a ballpoint pen. It had a metal clip to attach to a shirt pocket. He touched the tip of his finger to the roller-ball

1

applicator and glanced up at me suspiciously. I shrugged my shoulders, and he turned away.

He opened my cinnamon-flavored Blistex, my Advanced Formula Krazy Glue, my waxed CVS Dental Tape and my styptic pencil, and he sniffed my prescription-strength Cruex cream (for jock itch). I also had a small bottle of Listerine in the bag, an Arrid XX Ultra Clear Anti-Perspirant & Deodorant Solid and one NaturaLamb condom.

He did not open the Tic Tac box in which I store my emergency medications—aspirin, Motrin, sinus pills and laxatives—and did not ask me why I had three half-used toothpaste tubes, two travel toothbrushes, two Gillette Mac 3 razors and one Schick disposable razor. I couldn't have answered. I just put things in this kit spontaneously, whenever it occurs to me that I might need them. I always try to be prepared.

This is a very small, black canvas shaving kit by Edge Creek, which manufactures compact equipment for backpackers. It has three parts that fold into a bulky little package about the size of a paperback pocket dictionary. Unfolded, it has a hook to hang on a tree branch, and a tiny mirror to use for shaving.

Not that this man cared about the origin of the kit or the reasons for any of its contents. In light of the September 11 catastrophes at the World Trade Center and the Pentagon and in Somerset County, Pa., he had a suddenly high-profile job to do—a responsibility completely unrelated to revealing anything about my identify, other than the search for contraband that could endanger my fellow passengers or alter in any way the safe completion of my flight.

But I couldn't help feeling, as I stood at the table near the security area with people waiting behind me to have their own bags checked and simultaneously observing what I had in mine, that my life was now an open book and that I had somehow lost a significant measure of my privacy and dignity.

Of course we have all been faced with a foreboding and growing sense of loss since the horror of September 11, and I don't intend to compare the minor indignity I suffered at LaGuardia to the major devastation of those who lost lives, loved ones or livelihoods.

But every day since September 11, we have discovered ways in which our daily lives and the freedoms we have taken for granted have been substantially altered by Osama bin Laden and his death-squad fanatics. Extra security and delays at airports are more than minor annoyances: They are symbols of an increasingly altered and dangerous world. Our feelings of safety and comfort are forever diminished.

I was fortunate to know only two people directly affected by this horrible tragedy. Fred is a high-ranking executive in a major international financial institution with a large Wall Street facility. Lynn, his wife, is an artist whose bold canvases electrify their sprawling, high-tech Tribeca loft.

The first plane literally buzzed their loft before crashing into the WTC. Lynn was in the shower and heard the sickening sound of collision. She said to her husband, "Something terrible must have happened down in the street." He went to the window and then shouted for her to come running.

They sat on their living-room sofa, screaming and weeping and watching tiny figures—real people—leaping out of windows 60 stories above the street, with American Airlines Flight 11 hanging precariously from the WTC, piercing the heart of the financial district. Friends from neighboring lofts joined them. Together they witnessed the second collision and experienced the paralyzing and petrifying horror of the blitzkrieg.

Later, as survivors covered with inches of searing ash fled the devastation, Lynn and Fred rushed into the street and escorted the dazed victims into their apartment so they could wash themselves and call their families. Soon after the buildings collapsed, the water that came from their tap turned brown.

Writing in the New York Times nearly three weeks afterward, N.R. Kleinfeld talked about the aroma of the ash and of the ceaselessly smoldering buildings. "It's the odor of a burning computer. Or a burning tire. Or burning paper," Kleinfeld observed. "One person said it was the scent of unsettled souls."

When I visited Ground Zero that week, the aroma continued to pervade the air. It clung to my lungs like a living organism. Now, weeks later, I can still feel it, a scratching, haunting residue of those innocent victims whose lives were stolen from their children, families and countries. It is a tragedy and a crime that reverberates far beyond the barricades and the police and National Guard checkpoints surrounding the crime-scene perimeter.

Kleinfeld said, "A few people had their jacket collars pressed against their noses. A few others had tied handkerchiefs around their faces, bandit style. One young man simply pinched his nose with his fingers as he walked. A middle-aged woman had folded an American flag over her mouth."

This searing, sensory grimness is shared—and embraced—daily by a hoard of observers. The day I visited, tourists were pointing and clicking disposable cameras at the smoldering ruins partially concealed by Dumpsters and dump trucks. Police and National Guard in camouflage were everywhere, as were the media—notebooks in hand. TV reporters stood on makeshift platforms so the rubble could be seen behind them as they talked.

Paralleling the aroma, an all-pervading quiet hung in the air. In contrast to the usual noisy cacophony of New York—a symphony of horns, trucks, traffic, hucksters, cell phones and people shouting to be heard over every distraction—there was a startling edge of restraint. The boldness that characterizes city life was missing at Ground Zero and virtually everywhere else I visited in the city.

Earlier that day at Café Europa, a favorite midtown morning haunt across from Carnegie Hall, the wait staff were unusually friendly, greeting me as if I were a long-lost friend, though I am certain they hardly remembered me. They presented a free chocolate cookie with my portobello sandwich. A man in a purple sweater, yellow jacket and silk scarf sang to the music, smiling warmly over his tuna-salad sandwich. It occurred to me that I had never heard music at Café Europa before, perhaps because the place was usually mobbed at breakfast and lunch. Now, at 11:45 a.m., there were just six patrons.

I won't soon forget the scene at Europa or the aroma of which Kleinfeld writes, the water turning brown in Lynn and Fred's loft or the crusts of ash clinging to the people stumbling from the wreckage —not only because the reality of the experience is so stark, but also because the images are so specific and intimate.

This is a lesson that writers of all genres need to know—that the secret to making prose and poetry memorable and therefore vital and important is to catalog with specificity the details that are most intimate. By *intimate* I mean ideas and images that readers won't easily imagine —ideas and images you observed that symbolize a memorable truth about the characters or the situations that concern you.

In the introduction to his breakthrough 1973 anthology, "The New Journalism," Tom Wolfe writes about how Jimmy Breslin, a columnist for the New York Herald Tribune, captured the realistic intimacy of experiences by noticing details that could act as metaphors for something larger and more all-encompassing that he wanted to say.

Wolfe describes Breslin's coverage of the trial of Anthony Provenzano, a union boss charged with extortion. At the beginning, Breslin introduces the image of the bright morning sun bursting through the windows of the courtroom and reflecting off the large diamond ring on Provenzano's chubby pinky finger. Later, during a recess, Provenzano, flicking a silver cigarette holder, paces the halls, sparring with a friend who came to support him, the sun still glinting off the pinky ring.

Wolfe writes:

> *The story went on in that vein with Provenzano's Jersey courtiers circling around him and fawning while the sun explodes off his pinky ring. Inside the courtroom itself, however, Provenzano starts getting his. The judge starts lecturing him and the sweat starts breaking out on Provenzano's upper lip. Then the judge sentences him to seven years, and Provenzano starts twisting his pinky finger with his right hand.*

The ring is a badge of Provenzano's ill-gotten gains, symbolic of his arrogance and his eventual vulnerability and resounding defeat.

Although we can't achieve such symbolism each time we capture an incident, writers who want their words to be remembered beyond the date on which their stories are published or broadcast will seek to capture the special observations that symbolize the intimacy to which they have been exposed.

The details the security guard revealed about me by unpacking my shaving kit in front of a half-dozen strangers were not so shockingly intimate, but they were specific and revealing. You can piece together snatches of who I am and the way I am by thinking about my flashlight, my Itch Eraser, my Cruex and my triple toothbrushes and razors.

It is true that I am a bit absent-minded and also somewhat cautious. I back myself up with flashlights and salves so as to avoid situations that may annoy me or curtail my activities. If I confessed these traits to you in an essay, you would not necessarily find them memorable, but now, with the specifics of my shaving kit, a porthole into my personality has been revealed.

The earlier flight I had hoped to make was boarding when I was finally released by the security guard, and I rushed to see if I could get on. But I suddenly stopped to consider: It was at a gate that I had never used at LaGuardia for a Pittsburgh flight. I had used this gate to go to Washington, D.C., to Baltimore and Boston, but never Pittsburgh.

The flight was open. I could have gotten on and arrived back home to see my 10-year-old son before he went out with his mother. If I waited, I might not see him until the following morning when he returned to my house. But something told me the vibes weren't right. For no reason whatsoever, except for the gnawing feelings of foreboding inside me, I knew I shouldn't take that flight.

So I retreated to the U.S. Airways Club, nibbled on snack mix, sipped coffee for 90 minutes and stared out the window. My flight departed from Gate 12—the gate I almost always use when flying from LaGuardia to Pittsburgh—and I felt a lot better about traveling. Needless to say, nothing eventful occurred on the earlier flight—I checked when I got back to Pittsburgh—but now you know something else about me. I am cautious, but above all else, I listen to my instincts, no matter how illogical they may seem.

Why did I go to New York in the first place? Because I felt compelled to get on a plane in order to break the spell of hesitation and alienation cast by September 11. Normally I am on the road for a day nearly every week, but after September 11, I remained in my neighborhood for more than a month. It was time to see my friends and to experience New York, to understand that in almost every respect it was the same city as before—more sober, wounded and scarred, but inherently unbreakable.

The essays published in this issue also, like New York, represent survival and change, expressed through dramatic stories and intimacy of detail. In "Second Chances," Melissa Bloch, a breast-cancer survivor, is off on her own quest to Vietnam with a crew of plastic surgeons, while Philip Gerard's journey, "Adventures in Celestial Navigation," captures the intimacy of sailing and seeing blindly at night. Aine Greaney travels with her father on a mission of connection and maturity through a sensory panorama of Ireland. In "Bridges," Sarah Massey-Warren thrusts her readers into the stark and vivid reality of Elko, Nev., while Russell Tomlin, in "Two Years," leads us into Togo, West Africa, on a Peace Corps mission.

Jennifer Jeanne Patterson's "White Girl in Harlem" daringly captures the author's paranoia and helpless bigotry, while the intimate details reported by Ruthann Robson in "Notes on My Dying" capture the fear, heartbreak and confusion of her own impending death.

An interesting offshoot of this issue: While our associate editor, Tracy Ekstrand, was involved in our upcoming Diversity Issue, we turned to Susan Messer for help with copyediting. Her "Dots on the Page" is about the challenge and process—and details—of copyediting. The use of specific and significant details in writing and teaching, especially in relation to the events of September 11, is also discussed in Rose Toubes' column in the Between the Lines section of this issue.

The September 11 tragedy has delayed the publication of the JPMorgan Chase–sponsored Diversity Issue until March 2002. The winner of the $10,000 Walter Shipley Award, however, should be announced by the end of the year. We have also introduced a vehicle for expression and a forum for clearly articulated ideas about September 11 and its broad and unceasing impact by establishing an online "Living Issue." See http://www.creativenonfiction.org/livingissue for details.

Notes on My Dying

Ruthann Robson

I believe in death with dignity, don't you? At least in the abstract.

Grace. Nobility. Even beauty.

As abstract as that.

As abstract as other people.

As abstract as characters in fiction.

"All anyone wants is a good death," I read. This is in a short story. It's a prize-winning story, a story about a nurse who is dying of cancer. She is graceful, noble and even beautiful.

I hate the story. I hate stories about people dying of cancer, no matter how graceful, noble or beautiful.

When I read the author's note, I learn that he is an administrator in the famous cancer center where I am enduring chemotherapy and the news that I am going to die very shortly.

This is what I say to his story: I do not want your good death.

This is what I say to his biography: You make your living off other people's deaths.

This is what I insist: I am not your story.

If I were constructing this as a story, with myself as the protagonist, I would be not only dignified; I would be brave and beautiful, courageous and kind, humorous and honorable.

I would enshrine myself in narrative.

But this cannot be a success because the elements of narrative are corrupted.

There is no beginning. The beginning is not diagnosis. The beginning is before that. Before the suspicions, before the reconstructed past when one began to feel this or that, before everything except a tiny cell that got twisted and frisky. The absence of the beginning is compounded by the middle collapsing into the past.

Everything is end.

Some endings are longer than others.

I am trying to act as if I have a future.

When I'm not too weak, I go to work. I go to the library and the post office. I go for walks. And when I am too weak, I go anyway. The worst that could happen to me is already happening.

I cannot pretend I am who I was a few months ago, so I pretend I am a fashion model. I am a Buddhist nun with a shaved head. I am anorexic. I have a lovely pallor. I have a noble beauty, a beautiful nobility.

I am not interested in fooling anyone except myself.

I call it survival.

I survived a dangerous adolescence.

In school, the sentiments of "Death Be Not Proud" belied its title. On the large and small screens, "Love Story" jerked tears, and the body bags and the immolated monks screamed for my attention. In the streets and bathrooms, needles in the arm and suicide sang their romantic dirges.

Not all of us made it.

When I made it to 21, I assumed I would live to 87.

Death was for the young. And the old.

At 26, I was hospitalized intermittently for six weeks with a strange malady that spiked my temperature to 107 degrees.

"You should be dead," the doctor said, confirming my temperature.

"I'm not," I replied, thinking myself witty.

The year was 1984.

I was sure I had AIDS.

Instead, I was diagnosed with pesticide poisoning, contracted from the sugarcane fields where the migrant farm workers who were my clients worked.

A nurse told me I should be grateful for the advancement of antibiotics.

No one told me I should be irate about the development of agribusiness.

I knew I had almost died.

I thought I was cured.

There are those who argue that cancer is ancient, prevalent now only because other diseases have been cured and humans live longer, and unconnected to environmental degradation.

My body knows differently.

But who is there to blame? Industrialization? Capitalism? Corporate greed?

Anger is the second stage of dying in the classic work of Elisabeth Kübler-Ross. She notes that dying can cause a "usually dignified" person to act "furious," but with a bit of tolerance by the caregivers, the patient's anger can be soothed. Dying people, above all, want to be heard.

I do not want to be heard.

I do not want to talk.

I want to live.

My first decision about dying is that I will die at home. I will have the control and comfort I would not have in a hospital. The winter sun will be weak but brilliant, sifting through my window, refracting through a prism I have had since I was young. Then the light will fade, leaving only a slat of brilliant pink. Twilight was once my favorite time of day.

My second decision about dying is that I won't. Like all my most outrageous ambitions, it first appears on my horizon as a question: What if? What if I refused to die? I am neither stupid nor naive and know that it isn't a simple matter of choice. Nevertheless, my aspiration persists.

The first stage of dying is denial.

Ask anyone who has read Elisabeth Kübler-Ross.

Or who has not.

Still, what if I refused to cooperate?

The manifestations of my resistance are illogical and small. I refuse Ensure, Ativan, a port, a wig. I refuse to talk to my oncologist, who warns me about depression. Depression, the fourth stage of dying, is the "preparatory grief that the terminally ill patient has to undergo in order to prepare himself for his final separation from this world."

If I were talking to her, I would tell her I am not depressed, though I may seem defeated, decimated.

I am simply deep.

I am inside myself so deeply the world is an abstraction. I cannot bridge the distance between myself and everyone else, including the ones I love most. The ones I said I loved more than life itself. Now, this is no longer true.

My death is only my own. No matter the connection, no matter the love. No matter that I came from the bodies of my parents or that my child came from my body or that my lover and I have joined as if we inhabit one body without boundaries. Each body lives separately. And dies separately. Perhaps I knew this before. In the abstract.

I think about taking someone with me.

If I'm going to die anyway, shouldn't I kill someone? Shouldn't my death be useful? I scan my personal life but find no one evil enough to deserve to die. My passions are faded. I concentrate on the person I once hated most but cannot seem to despise him enough to deprive him of his narrow, miserable life.

Assassination is a possibility. I imagine buying a semi-automatic weapon. I have enough time for the license waiting period, to learn how to shoot, to do the legwork necessary to find a gap in the security. I think it would be relatively easy, since I'm not worried about getting caught. I would prefer not to die in prison, so I guess I'd kill myself as soon as my deed is done. I settle on a certain Supreme Court justice. But I find I don't care enough to kill him. Or even to think about it more than once.

Dying is lonely.

I am popular in my dying. People I have not heard from in several years call me.

"Is there anything you want to say to me?" she asks. She is crying.

"My mother died of cancer," he says to me. He must think this is an expression of empathy.

"You have always meant so much to me," she blurts. She does not stumble over the past tense.

I never respond.

They must think I am being dignified.

Someone actually tells me this: "I really admire the way you are conducting yourself with such dignity," she says to me.

"I'm not."

"Well, it seems like that to us," she persists. She is a colleague and has always been comfortable speaking for everyone at work.

"That's not the way it seems to me." I prove I can still argue.

She smiles as if she thinks I am being modest.

I am not.

I am trying to be honest: I am all claws and sobs and vomit. I am small and getting smaller. I am bereft and bald. I am more tired than tired.

How could she not see that when she looks at me?

But she does see that. Despite the dignity, when she looks at me, she sees I am dying.

And when I look at her, I see my dying reflected back to me, a shiny, silvery object without form or function, an abyss of pity.

I am grateful for the people who do not pity me. Or at least who do not show their pity.

We have written letters for almost 20 years. When I write to tell her the news that I am dying, I ask her to try to write to me as she always has, to write to me about her life and what she is reading. She writes me every day. Every single, fucking day. Beautiful, exquisitely boring letters about her job or what she ate for breakfast or something she hopes will be amusing. I live for her letters.

We have written letters for eight years. I fudge the fact that I am dying but also ask her to keep writing to me as she always has. Her letters get longer. Pages and pages, which require extra postage, pages filled with assessments of novels, pages brimming with struggles about her own writing, pages of poetry. I reread every page until I believe that I am strong enough to write back.

We have never written letters. She sends me a card. "Here's a second opinion: You're the greatest." It's in a package of gourmet food that once would have been appetizing.

We have lived together for more years than I can count. She was once my lover; now she is my caretaker. She tries not to cry in my presence. I am not so considerate.

She brings me books from the library when I can't get there myself. "Novels," I tell her, "from the New Fiction section." Sometimes she brings me the same book twice. Three times. Sometimes I recognize when this has happened.

Maybe I believe I can save myself through reading. Or at least escape. Or maybe it is that I have always read. Books were my first acquaintance with grace.

Although soon I stop reading fiction. I know she is screening the selections, but death penetrates the pages. Sometimes it is in the prize-winning story. Sometimes it is there casually and without warning. It seems there is always a convenient cancer death in the background somewhere, even if only in a character's memory.

In novels, they never recover.

Loss. Grieving. But life goes on.

I close the book and reach for the next one.

Soon I am requesting biographies. As if I have forgotten that the person in the biography is going to die. As if I didn't know somehow that Rachel Carson died at 57 of cancer. She hid it from the world, as if her dying were a recrimination of her work linking toxins with tumors in humans, an irrefutable rebuke that she was less than objective. Or perhaps she was trying to be dignified.

Desperation is not dignified.

Perhaps that is why Kübler-Ross does not name desperation as a stage. There is bargaining, the third stage, but she gives it short shrift. She theorizes it as a belief in a reward for good behavior. She doesn't seem to understand the will to live.

It allows the decision to be strapped into a chair and have poison injected into my veins seem rational.

It propels me into the alleys of alternative healing, alternative theories, alternative alternatives. I visualize and vitaminize. I spread myself on the floor of an apartment in Chinatown so that a man can bruise my flesh as a way of clearing my meridians. I ingest herbs from different continents, animal parts pressed into pill form, teas that smell like mentholated piss.

I meditate.

There are those who argue that cancer is a message: Appreciate the beauty of each moment.

The moments most often invoked are populated with children. What could be more precious than the kiss of a toddler?

Other moments to be cherished occur in nature: oceans, sunsets, trees and their turning leaves.

Even a circumscribed life has its moments to be appreciated. The soft sheets of the bed, the taste of a strawberry, the flames in the fireplace.

Never mentioned are the moments in which I am managing to live. The moments, long and slow, during which I am dizzy and puking red on the bathroom floor, trying to appreciate the texture and temperature of the tile against my cheek. (How smooth! How cool!) The moments, as panic-filled as a fire, when I feel the chemical burn in my veins and watch the skin on my arm lose all its color. The moments, shallow and distant, when I try to think about anything other than what is happening to me.

Acceptance is the fifth and final stage of dying, according to Kübler-Ross. She warns that the harder the struggle to avoid the inevitable death, and the more denial, the more difficult it will be to reach acceptance with peace and dignity. In her examples, the patient wants to die, but the medical professionals believe it is better to prolong life.

This is not my experience.

My medical professionals are very accepting of my death. They proclaim it inevitable and do not deny or struggle. They do not seem to believe it is better to prolong my life. They are very noble.

Perhaps they read Kübler-Ross in medical school. Or perhaps they're simply burnt out. Or they know the grim statistics for my rare cancer and see no reason why I should be in the smallest of minorities who might survive.

I loot the world for survival stories. Not the narratives of Himalayan treks or being lost at sea, but illness. The bookstore has an entire section on diseases and five shelves on cancer. I inspect every title, except the "prevention" ones, looking for possibilities. I buy a book by a Christian fundamentalist woman who attributes her survival to prayer and coffee enemas. I buy a book by a scientist who attributes his survival to vitamins. I buy books on healing by popular writers who intersperse their homilies with anecdotes of people given "six months to live" but who are alive 10 years later.

Possibilities.

I do not want nobility or beauty.

I do not want a good death.

I want possibility.

I am in my office, looking at the diplomas on my wall and sobbing over all that accomplishment, now utterly worthless. The skills I had mastered are the wrong skills for my situation. I know no medicine; my last biology class was in ninth grade. I can't even cope; my degrees are not in psychology or divinity. I learned how to think, how to read, how to argue.

My faith—in hard work, in intellectual pursuits, in books—has been misplaced. Nothing I know could save me. I want to rip my diplomas from the wall.

With dignity.

But I don't have the strength to carry a single book down the hall to the classroom. I can't stand up more than three and a half minutes. I no longer have the ability to assassinate that Supreme Court justice or to recall which one I had singled out as especially dastardly.

Still, I refuse to accept I am dying. I prefer denial, anger and even desperation.

When I can sit up, I spend hours at the computer, leaving no Web site unturned. I become an expert in my rare type of cancer. A medical dictionary replaces my thesaurus.

I read books, articles, pamphlets. I have begun to eschew fiction. I want true stories of survival. I relish attacks on statistics and science.

I avoid all eulogies, all obituaries. I do not update my will or think about the existence of my property without me. I don't care what happens to those hundreds of letters, the ones I have written or the ones I have read. I don't worry about my office and its diplomas. I am not interested in any legacy.

I try to think. To argue.

There are those who argue that cancer is an infectious disease, like tuberculosis, because a gene-based disease would have been eliminated through natural selection. Cancer could be cured by the correct antibiotic.

I would like this to be true.

Now.

I had thought I had looked at death before. I had seen her dance with the ones I loved who have died. I had suffered my own flirtations. This time, though, death is gazing back. Not just a glance, but a full, seductive stare. As if we are in a bar and I am dressed in black leather, ready for adventure tinged with danger.

How alluring to be chosen.

This is what she whispers: I can follow her with grace and dignity. Or I can resist and it can get ugly. Either way, she will win, she promises me.

That is her story.

If she writes my story, I will be brave, beautiful and dignified. The word *struggle* will be used but with no incidents of sweating or cursing or thrashing. In her story, it will be as if I have fallen into a deep sleep.

As long as I am still able to write, this is my story: I resist the lure of dignity; I refuse to be graceful, beautiful and beloved. I am not going to sleep with her. I'm going home alone.

Back to my books, my computer, my Australian herb and shark cartilage, my visualizations, meditations and bruised meridians. Back to my bedroom with the prism at twilight. Back to my office and its useless diplomas.

Back to my life.

Ruthann Robson *is on the board of www.sarcoma.net, a Web site devoted to the rare cancer of sarcoma, with which she was diagnosed in 1998 and from which she is now in remission. She is a professor of law at the City University of New York School of Law and has written widely on lesbian legal theory, including "Sappho Goes to Law School" (Columbia Univ. Press 1998). She also is the author of several novels, including "A/K/A" (St. Martin's Press 1998).*

Dots on the Page

Susan Messer

*W*hen I teach my copyediting class, I begin with the story of Dick Dick and Judy Dick. I tell this story because it is one way to explain the roots of my interest in the tiny details of language as they sit on the page. I want my students to reflect on the roots of their own interest in language on the page, and thus, on what brought them to this class in the first place. And I want them to do it right away. So here is my opening story:

When I was just learning to read, I had a book about a brother and sister named Dick and Judy. Not Dick and *Jane*—I always say—but Dick and Judy. One night, I sat on the couch in my living room, attempting to read this book. I must have had the concept of words by then but not the concept of sentences, because this is more or less what I saw:

Here comes Dick Dick is a boy

Here comes Judy Dick is her brother

I read these words again and again, and they didn't make sense. Why did the boy have the same first and last name? And why was Judy Dick someone's brother? And the more I tried to understand—the repetitive names, the odd relationships—the more frustrated I became. I must have screamed or thrown the book across the room, because one of my parents came to the rescue and asked what was wrong.

"Why are these people called Dick Dick and Judy Dick?" I demanded. "None of this makes sense."

The rescuing parent recognized the problem and explained punctuation: The little dots on the page are important. Each marks the end of a unit; when you see one, you pause and then go on to the next idea, like this:

Here comes Dick. Dick is a boy.

Here comes Judy. Dick is her brother.

When I heard that, I felt a warm glow of understanding—and wonder—that a tiny dot of ink could unlock meaning on the page.

When I finish telling this story in my copyediting class, I let the students sit with these thoughts for a few moments, and then I go right on to another story—about an editor I heard speak at a meeting of women in the publishing industry. When this editor was a little girl, she told us, she gained a reputation as the only person on her block who could untie knots in a necklace chain. The neighbors all came to her with their knots.

As she told her story, I noticed her long, slim fingers and the intense focus of her eyes, and I pictured her poring over a thin gold chain, rolling, analyzing and then teasing out the knot. She told this story because she thought it foreshadowed her career as an editor—one who unties knots in the chain of words. And this in fact offers a good partial definition of *copyediting*. Here's another one, which I wrote for the brochure that advertises my course:

> *Copyediting is a process of close reading and editing with a focus on the mechanics of language, the author's and publisher's style and the manuscript's substance. Like the ballet dancer's six positions and the musician's scales, the copyeditor's techniques provide fluidity and consistency in the finished work.*

And here's another, as presented in the mighty Chicago Manual of Style, 14th Edition, the 921-page text from the University of Chicago Press:

> *The editorial function is in effect two processes. The first, because it is concerned with the mechanics of written communication, may be called* mechanical editing. *The process involves a close reading of the manuscript with an eye to such matters as consistency of capitalization, spelling, and hyphenation; agreement of verbs and subjects, and other matters of syntax; punctuation; beginning and ending quotation marks and parentheses; number of ellipses points; numbers given as numerals or spelled out; and many similar details of style. ... The second editorial process may be called* substantive editing—rewriting, reorganizing, or suggesting other ways to present material.

So together, the two stories—of Dick Dick and Judy Dick and the knots in the chain—describe the two parts of the process, mechanical and substantive.

Copyediting is not appropriately respected in this world—not even by me—as evidenced by the fact that I always quickly point out to my class that "I don't do much copyediting anymore." Though of course I do. It's a foundation for everything from evaluating a manuscript to writing one.

I once heard Ray Charles interviewed on "All Things Considered" —in honor of his 67th birthday. Robert Siegel asked him whether he still practiced piano, and Charles answered yes. Then the conversation went something like this:

"Do you practice *songs?*" Siegel asked.

"No no no no no no no no no," Charles answered. I pictured him shaking his head back and forth vigorously.

"I take it the answer is no," Siegel noted.

Charles laughed, then explained: "The songs I already know," he said. "What I practice is my scales." It's the scale practice that keeps his fingers nimble enough to play the songs. The scales aren't exactly music, the ballet positions aren't exactly dance, and the mechanics of language aren't exactly literature, but without them, you're naught.

Still, copyediting is one of the lower-status tasks in the publishing house (just above proofreading) and one of the lowest paid. It's the workhorse of literature. And yet, some people do want to learn and practice the discipline of copyediting, so they come to my class. They come for various reasons: They want to gain a practical skill they can use to earn money; they have a job in which they need the skills; they are writers and wish to polish things up in their work. So, despite my ambivalence, I argue for the importance of these small matters of language and how they add up to something very grand.

But now it's time for my students to do some hands-on work, so I ask them to turn to our first exercise: a list of 20 simple sentences, each with at least one error, that we'll study together. I want them to detect the error, say what *kind* of error it is, and suggest an improvement or correction. The students like this, although some are better than others at finding the errors, and most find it difficult to give them names. I want them to be able to name the errors for a few reasons: (1) they may have to name them for the author whose work they edit, to justify a suggested change; (2) knowing the name (redundancy, mis-placed modifier, punctuation, lack of parallelism) will help them find support or guidance in a style manual—that is, they'll know what to look for in the table of contents or index; and (3) knowing the names is a way of deconstructing the skills of the copyeditor, of recognizing what it takes to do the work. But after we've gone through all 20 sentences, each illustrating another potential trap, some students are wondering whether it's time to drop out of this class, so I try to elevate them.

I read them a letter to the editor from Poets & Writers, the July/August 1997 issue:

Flaunt or Flout?

I hate to be cranky and anal [copyeditors and upholders of language rules and standards are often accused of both], but as a writer—and one who teaches English composition for a living...—I would like to be able to depend on P&W for, at least, accuracy and reasonable correctness, and in your March/April issue, I find neither.

Specifically, on page 61 you quote interviewee Octavia Butler "On Other Writers": "As a kid, I also read a lot of Felix Sultan." Now, Butler may have spelt the name incorrectly to, or for, your interviewer, but surely someone at the office checks these things?

The author of "Bambi" is Felix Salten: SALTEN. I enjoyed the rest of the interview (and consequently, do plan to read Butler's oeuvre) but still...

Again, on page 81, an otherwise interesting and informative article on poet Robert Law notes that "Merton and Law, admirers of James Joyce's 'Finnegans Wake,' regularly flaunted rules of spelling, capitaliza-tion, and punctuation." The confusion of flaunted with flouted is perhaps the result of a culture-wide imprecision of language, and not necessarily of ignorance, but again, unless Law and Merton were holding up placards emblazoned with such legends as "I before E except after C" and "Never Use a Comma to Connect Two or More Independent Clauses," I believe flouted is the correct choice in this instance.

I leave you with this thought, courtesy of Edwin Newman: "Those for whom words have lost their meaning are likely to find that ideas have also lost their meaning." Thank you—and keep up the (mostly) good work.

Gina Logan
Northfield, Vermont

This matter of Sultan versus Salten reminds me to tell my students another story—one on the subject of checking things and the self-discipline needed by the copyeditor. I sometimes copyedit for River Oak Review, a literary magazine published in Oak Park, Ill. Once, I got a story to copyedit—a really good one—that included the names of both Jascha Heifetz and Yehudi Menuhin. I loved this story, especially its bizarre characters and weird, dreamy tone, and it almost lulled me into a trance.

Gradually, however, I became aware of an annoying seed of anxiety sprouting within me. I ignored it until the feeling took shape in words:

"Now hold on," it said. "You don't have any idea how to spell those violinists' names."

Which was true. And begrudgingly, I confessed that it was, after all, my job to make sure they were right. So I got out my Webster's 10th Collegiate dictionary, turned to the biographical names section at the end (students are rarely aware that this section exists), and discovered that *both* names had been spelled wrong (*Jascha* misspelled as *Jasha*, and *Menuhin* misspelled as *Menuin*). So. Though I had the frustration of detaching from the story to nitpick at it, I also had the satisfaction of what some copyeditors call "a good catch" and what others call "a fix."

I hate to be cranky and anal (or do I?), but even if only one reader noticed the misspelled names, that would be too many. And for that person, the credibility of the whole journal might be undermined.

Now I take this story of Jascha Heifetz and Yehudi Menuhin apart for my students and show what's involved: the instinct to know what you don't know, the discipline to stop, the awareness of what resources you have for finding the answers. The first two I teach through stories and exercises; the last one, the resources, we'll cover in a later class on style manuals and dictionaries.

But now, since the students are looking glum about all those land-mines scattered across the pages, I turn to volume 22 of the Missouri Review, the "Altered States" volume from 1999, to an essay called "A Yankee Fan in the Floating World," by Melanie Hammer. I read from the second paragraph:

> *I had majored in English, but it turned out to be even more useful that I had excelled at typing in junior high. I landed a job as an editorial assistant at a university press and set about the business of becoming a*

grown-up. My two bosses treated me as if I were bright enough, one in particular reminding me that she had started off as an editorial assistant herself. They acquired books, and I typed their correspondence with a variety of authors. They had interesting jobs, but I liked it better over in copyediting, a warren where women in glasses polished text like old silver, working in the intricacies of language until they brought it to a shine.

When I came across this passage the first time, I got the same warm glow I got from my Dick Dick and Judy Dick experience. This time it came from the spotlight that Hammer focused on the intricacies, the caretaking, the devotion to keeping something beautiful.

Not everyone may like the image, though. First, many people don't like to polish silver. I don't. I have a fabulous art deco tea and coffee set, inherited from my mother, but I store it in the basement, wrapped in special soft cloths, because I can't keep up with the job. The gleaming surface tarnishes almost as soon as I've finished polishing.

Second, the image from Hammer's essay is both domestic and female, an uneasy alliance for many these days. It is true, however, that most copyeditors are women. And most of my students are women. Here, I think about but don't read from the insightful but troubling essay by Megan L. Benton, from the July 1992 issue of Scholarly Publishing. The essay is called "A Voice from the Margins: Women, Editing, and Publishing Education." Listen to Benton:

The diminishment of editing is also diminishment of women's work, perhaps in part because it is women's work. Manuscript editing is predominantly done by women, of course; in fact, it offers an almost classical profile of both the sociological and the psychological aspects of so-called women's work. In the latter sense, young girls are commonly groomed for the kind of subordinate, silent task of "tidying up" another's work that editing entails, for work whose "only aim is to make the writer look as good as possible" [endnote omitted]. ... Most standard textbook introductions to copy editing caution novices to suppress their taste, their style, their opinions.

So. Not only cranky and anal, but self-effacing, nurturing silver polishers—engaged in an art and a craft that the world rarely recognizes or acknowledges. And while it's the women who do the work, it is the men—H. W. Fowler, William Safire, Theodore Bernstein, Edwin Newman—whose names we know best.

But enough of this storytelling and philosophizing. The students have come to learn copyediting, so let's get on with it. Then, notice that although I spell copyediting as one word, Benton (or her copyeditor, most likely) spelled it as two. Which is right? The answer is *neither*. None of this stuff, I assure my students, is decreed by God (and even if it were, people might disagree). It's not like Jascha Heifetz and Yehudi Menuhin, where the violinists themselves (or their parents) can declare the one true spelling. So it depends. Which spelling does the publishing house prefer?

We hope it has rules for such matters, with specific examples, set out in a house style manual or style sheet, or that this style manual will tell the copyeditor where to refer for such questions. If the copyeditor is using the Chicago Manual of Style, she is told to refer to Webster's 10th for questions regarding spelling. So I do, and uh-oh, I see that in Webster's, *copy editor* is spelled as two words, but the verb *copyedit* is spelled as one. And now I look back to the index of the Chicago Manual and see that both *copyediting* and *copyeditor* are spelled as one word (or *closed up*, in copyediting lingo).

You may now say, "Who cares?" But if you *do* care—as do Gina Logan, Melanie Hammer and Megan L. Benton, here's what you do: You make a decision (*copy edit* or *copyedit*) and stick with it. Consistency, to the extent that it's possible without forcing a square peg into a round hole, is one goal of copyediting.

And some of the guidelines for establishing consistency are found in the Chicago Manual, in chapters 5–8: "Punctuation" (the tiniest ink dots on the page), "Spelling and Distinctive Treatment of Words" (more about this in a moment), "Names and Terms" (capitalization) and "Numbers" (whether you use numerals or spell them out).

When I first became an editor, chapter 6—"Spelling and Distinctive Treatment of Words"—was the oddest to me. I thought spelling was something you learned in grade school, and that was it. I knew that plenty of words are hard to spell, but then you look them up in the dictionary or use the spell check on your computer. But no. The Chicago Manual has just under 40 pages on the subject, full of concerns you never realized were concerns until they pointed them out to you:

> *A chapter on spelling in a style manual may disregard most of the dozens or hundreds of questions about spelling that arise in the course of*

Dots on the Page

writing or editing a serious book, for the answers may be found in a standard dictionary. There are some spelling matters, however, that a dictionary does not cover or on which its guidance is obscure [e.g., plurals (sergeants-at-arms, courts-martial), possessives (Kansas's not Kansas'), word divisions (democ-racy not demo-cracy)], and it is to these that the present chapter is addressed. . . . The chapter ends with a tabulation of some rules for spelling compound words.

That little "tabulation"—13 pages on proper use of hyphens—makes most people very uncomfortable, so I tell a story. I got my first job as an editor because I was a friend of the boss, and he knew I'd work hard even though I didn't know anything about editing. To prepare for the job, I studied a stack of grammar and editing books. In the process, I came across the concept of the hyphenated unit modifier, as in *low-income family.* In that phrase, the hyphen holds the first two words together and makes them into a unit that together modifies the third word. In some cases, I read in my books, the hyphen is essential to meaning, as in *light-blue hat* versus *light blue hat.* In the phrase with the hyphen we are clearly talking about color, a light shade of blue. Without the hyphen, the phrase is ambiguous: We could be talking about color *or* weight—as in a blue hat made of straw or cotton as opposed to wool or felt.

Perhaps the hyphen is not the best way to let the reader know (*Substitute* straw *or* cotton *if that's what you mean?* the editor might query diplomatically from the margin), but this concept made some sense to me. So in my first weeks on the new job, I used lots of hyphens, to show that I knew my way around.

One day, an editor down the hall—she'd been checking my work when I was done—came into my office, closed the door, and took a seat. She placed her fingers on her temples.

"Susan," she said, "You're *killing* me with hyphens."

I keep this quote in mind not only because I like it so much but also because it's so broadly relevant—especially in the context of being a beginner, overapplying a rule, and then being reined in. The Chicago Manual's tabulation can rein in the beginner who takes the time to penetrate its dense mysteries, and as I finish this story, I notice that my students are flipping through it, trying to do just that.

This can be a good time to mention the funny essay by Nicholson Baker from "The Best American Essays, 1994," called "Survival of the Fittest," which is in part about the history of punctuation. Baker is a writer who is preoccupied—okay, obsessed—with the details of modern life, and I like to read my students a few paragraphs from his essay, to show that we're not alone in our copyediting concerns.

> *American copy-editing [note the hyphen] has fallen into a state of demoralized confusion over hyphenated and unhyphenated compounds —or at least, I am demoralized and confused, having just gone through the manuscript of a novel in which a very smart and careful and good-natured copy-editor has deleted about two hundred of my innocent tinker-toy hyphens. I wrote "stet hyphen" in the margin so many times that I finally abbreviated to "SH"—but there is no wicked glee in my intransigence: I didn't want to be the typical prose prima donna who made her life difficult.*
>
> *On the other hand, I remembered an earlier manuscript of mine in which an event took place in the back seat of a car: in the bound galleys, the same event occurred in the "backseat." The* backseat. *Grateful for hundreds of other fixes, unwilling to seem stubborn, I had agreed without protest to the closing-up, but I stewed about it afterward and finally rein-serted a space before publication.... Therefore, mindful of my near miss with "back seat," I stetted myself sick over the new manuscript. I stetted* re-enter *(rather than* reenter*),* post-doc *(rather than* postdoc*),* foot-pedal *(rather than* foot pedal*),* second-hand *(rather than* secondhand*),* twist-tie *(rather than* twist tie*), and* pleasure-nubbins *(rather than* pleasure nubbins*).*

As I finish reading this excerpt, I'm pleased because some students are flipping through their Webster's to see what it has to say about *backseat*, and they find that indeed it is listed as one word, and Baker's copyeditor was "right."

"Nicholson," she might have said, if she was a scrappy one, "You're killing me with hyphens."

But as you know, the copyeditor's job—and often, her nature— is not to be scrappy. Also, Baker was the author, so his preferences generally override. The copyeditor retreats, "lets him have it" (his way, that is) and moves on. The point is not so much to win or lose any particular match, but to raise consciousness about the stylistic decisions one makes.

Chapter 7, on capitalization, is one of my favorites in the Chicago Manual, because though dizzying in specificity, it reveals much about the values in our culture and the importance we give to the details of language even without realizing it. This chapter (60 pages) sets out the basic problem:

> *Questions and differences of opinion arise over what constitutes a proper noun, other than the name of a person or place. It is with this realm of uncertainty that the following rules attempt to deal. They reflect the tendency toward the use of fewer capitals, toward what is called a down (lowercase) style as opposed to an up (uppercase, i.e., capital letter) style.*

The pages and lists of names and terms can't easily be summarized, but to exemplify this *down style,* I say to my students, "You don't capitalize *president* in president of the United States; you don't even capitalize *the pope.*" Of course, style and grammar books may differ on this point—on every point, for that matter. It all comes down to a panel of people making the decisions, and the decisions add up to a value system. At U-C Press, for example, the value is that a down style is preferable to an up one:

> *In few areas is an author more tempted to overcapitalize or an editor more loath to urge a lowercase style than in religion. ... this is probably due to unanalyzed acceptance of the pious customs of an earlier age, to an unconscious feeling about words as in themselves numinous, or to fear of offending religious persons.*

This fear of offending is prominent in many students' minds, and some tell me about the newsletters they produce at work, in which they have to capitalize everything—the President of the Board, the Assistant Vice President of Operations, the Chairman of the Department, the Director of Safety. If they don't, people get insulted. And of course, in this context, politics and job security win over U-C rules. But look at the core issue, I say: The appearance and height of a letter at the start of a word affects how people feel about their status and whether they're getting the proper respect. *Any better way to show how important you are?* the scrappy copyeditor might whisper from the margin.

Last time I taught my class, one clever student noted that according to the U-C capitalization principles, he should lowercase Dalai Lama (the term itself is not listed in the Manual), but he couldn't make himself do it. I'm with him. It seems to be a special situation, but I can't explain why. Words *are* numinous, at least certain ones.

By now, of course, we're into the third or fourth session in the copyediting course, and I've given the students lots of exercises to do at home. These exercises force them to explore the Chicago Manual, to use the editing marks (the squiggles that editors use to communicate), and to think like copyeditors. Much of the homework is excruciatingly picky and time-consuming, and many students complain about it. But these are all adults; they have the choice to do the homework or not (there's no grade in the course), and if they want to do it, they'll get lots of practice (remember Ray Charles) in the thing they came to learn. But I don't want them to get too down in the dumps and to *hate* the idea of copyediting, so I keep going with the stories.

One day they come in, and here's what I've written on the flip chart: *A jewel returned to it's owner.* I tell them that this is going to be a story about how copyediting skills are practical, and then I tell them that this line is *almost* the inscription that appeared on my mother's gravestone.

And, well, they don't know how to respond at all. First, they've just learned that my mother *has* a gravestone, and they want to respond with sympathy. Second, they're not sure what the line on the flip chart means. Third, some have recognized the grammatical error and want to point it out. Fourth, they don't know what I mean by *almost*; is it on the stone or not? They're torn between the meaning and the mechanics —good training for the copyeditor—so I push on with my story.

My father lived in Detroit, and he placed the order for my mother's gravestone after our family had together chosen the inscription. One weekend, my sister and I went to visit him, and he suggested that we go the stonecutter's to check the template for the stone before the cutting began.

The stonecutter took us into the dusty workroom, where he had a rubbery sheet stretched over the face of my mother's stone, with all the text drawn in, and then he left us to look at it. I pointed to the apostrophe in *it's*.

BUSINESS REPLY MAIL
FIRST CLASS MAIL   PERMIT NO. 17218-526   PITTSBURGH, PA

POSTAGE WILL BE PAID BY ADDRESSEE

CREATIVE NONFICTION
PO BOX 3000
DENVILLE NJ 07834-9259

BUSINESS REPLY MAIL
FIRST CLASS MAIL   PERMIT NO. 17218-526   PITTSBURGH, PA

POSTAGE WILL BE PAID BY ADDRESSEE

CREATIVE NONFICTION
PO BOX 3000
DENVILLE NJ 07834-9259

"That shouldn't be there," I said.

My father and sister weren't sure, so I gave an on-the-spot grammar lesson: *It's* is a contraction, standing for *it is*; here, the *'s* does not signal a possessive, as it usually does. The irregularity trips up many people; I've seen it in the manuscripts of Harvard professors—easy enough to excise with the editorial pen. Here, however, a cliché taking on literal meaning and about to be carved in stone.

Once my father and sister got my point, we hailed the stonecutter and told him the news. He argued: The apostrophe was needed. I argued back: It wasn't. He shook his head. I nodded mine.

My sister, tired of the argument, picked up a pen, went to the stone, and drew a big x through the apostrophe. The stonecutter winced—*You'll regret this.* But I didn't, and instead, I felt like some editorial superwoman, swooping in to save the day.

The students are impressed with this story, so it's a good time to give them something hard to do. On the course syllabus, I promised to tell about the dictionary. So I do. I start with an impossible spelling test. It's a list of about 30 words like *hors d'oeuvres, desiccate, deceased, innocuous, inoculate* and *millennium,* but many of them are spelled wrong (with too many or too few double letters, for example), and the students have to identify which ones and correct them. I don't really expect anyone to be able to do this. What I want to demonstrate is that spelling is hard, that our language is full of irregularities, and no one can know all of them. I explain also that our language is living, so it changes. That's why Webster's is in a 10th edition and will eventually be in an 11th. Words and meanings are added and dropped, and spellings change, or several spellings are acceptable, usually with the "preferred" spelling appearing first. Here's Webster's on the subject:

> *The writing system of Modern English allows for considerable variation, as is shown by the persistence of variant spellings like* veranda *and* verandah, *or* judgment *and* judgement *and by the fact that many compound words have solid, hyphenated, and open stylings all in common use currently (*decision maker, decision-maker, decisionmaker*). At the same time, however, it [the writing system] tends to be a force for standardization and unification because recorded language creates a precedent for future language use and provides a basis on which language use can be taught to the younger members of a community.*

But who determines the standard? Again, it's human beings. As invisible as copyeditors, a panel of linguists and scholars stands behind these small official-looking words on the dictionary page. They study and sift, respond to letters from users and do their best to interpret and uphold the trends and traditions.

"Webster's is our friend," I say. "I keep it on my desk almost all the time."

I show the students the dictionary's useful features—the biographical and geographical sections at the end and (my favorite) the synonym deconstructions and usage notes that follow selected words. Most students have never noticed these. So I ask them to look up, for example, *concise.* And there, they see an exposé of the subtle distinctions between *concise, terse, succinct, laconic, summary, pithy* and *compendious.* Once, I tell them, I left an author breathless by instructing him (thanks to American Heritage that time) on the differences between *summit, peak, pinnacle, climax, apex* and *acme.* The students are into their dictionaries now, so I move on to the usage notes.

"OK," I say, "let's discuss *between* and *among.*" Some (usually the younger students) look puzzled, and this surprised me the first time I taught the class.

"You never learned any rule?" I ask.

But those who did (usually the older students) are wedded to the rule they learned. In fact, I've found, it's one of the few grammar rules some students remember. And that's too bad, because I'm about to snatch their last shred of security. I ask them to read the usage note that appears at the entry for *between* ("There is a persistent but unfounded notion that *between* can be used only for two items...").

Though upsetting to their sense of language reality, once the students recover, they're empowered. They see where language authority comes from, and they see that rules are both useful and broken. And they start to see this, too:

It's a wrestling match. In one corner, the great powerhouse: the living language, *numinous,* fighting for unshackled freedom. In the other corner, the cranky contender: a consortium of steadfast Webster's, the weighty style manuals and the front-line copyeditors—sparring for standards, consistency, precedents.

The opponents meet. They circle. They become a cycle, a cycloid, a cyclometer, a cyclone, a cyclops, a cyclotron. They collide.

And it's particles.

And the particles merge.

And they're dots.

And the dots rally.

They become signs and wonders: letters of many shapes and sizes.

The letters connect, align themselves in neat horizontals.

Spaces nuzzle in, detach units of meaning: words.

And the words cluster.

They gel into sentences, paragraphs.

Marks, short and tall, judiciously intercede to signal pauses, stops, questions.

And long, skillful fingers tease out the flow.

They unsnarl, hone, buff, query.

And meanwhile, in quiet places all across the world, our readers, blissfully unaware of all that commotion, settle in and look to the page.

Susan Messer *is a writer and editor who lives in Oak Park, Ill. Her fiction and nonfiction have appeared in* North American Review, River Oak Review *and the* Chicago Reader. *She has been a finalist in Glimmer Train's Very Short Fiction competition and the Chicago Tribune's Nelson Algren competition. One of her stories won Chicago Public Radio's Stories on Stage competition and was performed at the Museum of Contemporary Art, Chicago.*

Killing Chickens

Meredith Hall

I tucked her wings tight against her heaving body, crouched over her, and covered her flailing head with my gloved hand. Holding her neck hard against the floor of the coop, I took a breath, set something deep and hard inside my heart, and twisted her head. I heard her neck break with a crackle. Still she fought me, struggling to be free of my weight, my gloved hands, my need to kill her. Her shiny black beak opened and closed, opened and closed silently, as she gasped for air. I didn't know this would happen. I was undone by the flapping, the dust rising and choking me, the disbelieving little eye turned up to mine. I held her beak closed, covering that eye. Still she pushed, her reptile legs bracing against mine, her warmth, her heart beating fast with mine. I turned her head on her floppy neck again, and again, corkscrewing her breathing tube, struggling to end the gasping. The eye, turned around and around, blinked and studied me. The early spring sun flowed onto us through a silver stream of dust, like a stage light, while we fought each other. I lifted my head and saw that the other birds were eating still, pecking their way around us for stray bits of corn. This one, this twisted and broken lump of gleaming black feathers, clawed hard at the floor, like a big stretch, and then deflated like a pierced ball. I waited, holding her tiny beak and broken neck with all my might.

I was killing chickens. It was my 38th birthday. My brother had chosen that morning to tell me that he had caught his wife—my best friend, Ashley—in bed with my husband a year before. I had absorbed the rumors and suspicions about other women for 10 years, but this one, I knew, was going to break us. When I roared upstairs and confronted John, he told me to go fuck myself, ran downstairs and jumped into the truck. Our sons, Sam and Ben, were making a surprise for me at the table; they stood behind me silently in the kitchen door while John gunned the truck out of the yard. "It's okay, guys," I said. "Mum and Dad just had a fight. You better go finish my surprise before I come peeking."

I carried Bertie's warm, limp body outside and laid her on the grass. Back inside the coop, I stalked my hens and came up with Tippy-Toes. I gathered her frantic wings and crouched over her. John was supposed to kill off our beautiful but tired old hens, no longer laying, last month to make way for the new chicks that were arriving tomorrow. But he was never around, and the job had not been done. I didn't know how to do this. But I was going to do it myself. This was just a little thing in all the things I was going to have to learn to do alone.

I had five more to go. Tippy-Toes tried to shriek behind my glove. I clamped my hand over her beak and gave her head a hard twist. I felt her body break deep inside my own chest.

Two down. I felt powerful, capable. I could handle whatever came to me.

But I needed a rest. I was tired, exhausted, with a heavy, muffled weight settling inside. "I'm coming in," I called in a false, singsong voice from the kitchen door. "Better hide my surprise." Ten and 7, the boys knew something was up, something bigger than the moody, dark days John brought home, bigger than the hushed, hissing fights we had behind our bedroom door, bigger than the days-long silent treatment John imposed on me if I asked too many questions about where he had been and why. Sam and Ben were working quietly in the kitchen, not giggling and jostling the way they usually did. Their downy blond heads touched as they leaned over their projects. I felt a crush of sadness, of defeat. We were exploding into smithereens on this pretty March day, and we all knew it.

"I have to make a cake!" I sang from the doorway. "When are you guys going to be done in there?"

"Wait! Wait!" they squealed. It was an empty protest, their cheer as hollow as mine.

Our old house smelled good, of wood and the pancakes the three of us had eaten this morning, in that other world of hope and tight determination before my brother's phone call. We lived on a ridge high over the mouth of the Damariscotta River on the coast of Maine. From our beds, we could all see out over Pemaquid Point, over Monhegan Island, over the ocean to the edge of the Old World. The rising sun burst into our sleep each morning. At night, before bed, we lay on my bed together—three of us—naming Orion and Leo and the Pleiades in whispers. Monhegan's distant light swept the walls of our rooms all night at 36-second intervals. Our little house creaked in the wind during February storms. Now spring had come, and the world had shifted.

"Help me make my cake," I said to the boys. They dragged their chairs to the counter.

"Mum, will Dad be home for your birthday tonight?" Sam asked. Both boys were so contained, so taut, so helpless. They leaned against me, quiet.

Guilt and fear tugged me like an undertow. I started to cry.

"I don't know, my loves. I think this is a really big one."

Bertie and Tippy-Toes lay side by side on the brown grass, their eyes open, necks bent. I closed the coop door behind me and lunged for the next hen.

"It's all right," I said softly. "It's all right. Everything's going to be all right. Shhh, Silly, shh." I crouched over her. Silly was the boys' favorite because she let them carry her around the yard. I hoped they would forget her when the box of peeping balls of fluff arrived tomorrow.

"It's okay, Silly," I said quietly, wrapping my gloved fingers around her hard little head. She was panting, her eyes wild, frantic, betrayed. I covered them with my fingers and twisted her neck hard. Her black wings, iridescent in the dusty sunlight, beat against my legs. I held her close to me while she scrabbled against my strong hands. I started to cry again.

When I went back up to the house, Bertie and Tippy-Toes and Silly and Mother Mabel lay on the grass outside the coop.

Benjamin came into the kitchen and leaned against my legs. "What are we going to do?" he asked.

"About what, Sweetheart?" I hoped he was not asking me about tomorrow. Or the next day.

"Nothing," he said, drifting off to play with Sam upstairs.

We frosted the cake blue, Ben's favorite color, and put it on the table next to their presents for me, wrapped in wallpaper. I wanted to call someone, to call my mother or my sister. Yesterday I would have called Ashley, my best friend, who had listened to me cry and rail about John again and again. Instead, I brought in three loads of wood and put them in the box John had left empty.

"Sam, will you lay up a fire for tonight? And Ben, go down to the cellar and get a bunch of kindling wood."

Like serious little men, my children did what I asked.

"What are we going to make for my birthday supper?"

"I thought we were going to Uncle Stephen's and Aunt Ashley's," Sam said.

"Know what?" I said. "Know what I want to do? Let's just stay here and have our own private little party. Just us."

I felt marooned with my children. I sat at the table, watching while they did their chores, then headed back out to finish mine.

Minnie Hen was next. She let me catch her and kill her without much fight. I laid her next to the others in the cold grass.

Itty-Bit was last. She was my favorite. The others had chewed off her toes, one by one, when she was a chick. I had made a separate box for her, a separate feeder, separate roost, and smeared antibiotic ointment four times a day on the weeping stubs. She survived, and ate from my hand after that. She had grown to be fierce with the other hens, never letting them too close to her, able to slip in, grab the best morsels and flee before they could peck her. I had come to admire her very much, my tough little biddie.

She cowered in the corner, alone. I sat next to her, and she let me pull her up into my lap. I stroked her feathers smooth, stroke after stroke. Her comb was pale and shriveled, a sign of her age. I knew she hadn't laid an egg for months. She was shaking. I held her warmth against me, cooing to her, "It's all right, Itty Bit. Everything's going to be all right. Don't be scared." My anger at John centered like a tornado on having to kill this hen. "You stupid, selfish son of a bitch," I said. I got up, crying again, holding Itty-Bit tight to me. I laid her gently on the floor and crouched over her. The sun filled the coop with thick light.

That night, after eating spaghetti and making a wish and blowing out 38 candles and opening presents made by Sam and Benjamin—a mail holder made from wood slats, a sculpture of 2-by-4s and shells; after baths and reading stories in bed and our sweet, in-the-dark, whispered good nights; after saying "I don't know what is going to happen" to my scared children; after banking the fire and turning off the lights, I sat on the porch in the cold, trying to imagine what had to happen next. I could see the outline of the coop against the dark, milky sky. I touched my fingers, my hands, so familiar to me. Tonight they felt like someone else's. I wrapped my arms around myself— thin, tired—and wished it were yesterday.

Tomorrow morning, I thought, I have to turn over the garden and go to the dump. Tomorrow morning, I have to call a lawyer. I have to figure out what to say to Sam and Benjamin. I have to put Ben's sculpture on the mantel and put some mail in Sam's holder on the desk. I have to clean out the coop and spread fresh shavings.

Meredith Hall *lives and writes in Maine. She teaches writing at the University of New Hampshire.*

Second Chances

Melissa Bloch

Geoff, a plastic surgeon from Fort Wayne, is explaining to a Vietnamese surgeon and Mike, a fourth-year medical student from New Jersey, what he will do to the 5-year-old in front of him. The child's head is tipped back, eyes taped shut, fine black hair spread out, dirty feet and hands relaxed. The Dingman, a sort of metal mouth rack, has stretched him open like a gaping cavern. I look down inside him from above to see a natural wonder. The split lip leads to a winding path through the gums and down into a serpentine chasm banked by pink bony ridges, descending to a murky red pool in the child's throat.

My expectations for this volunteer medical mission had been vague, as were my reasons for going. The fervor that compelled me toward this adventure, however, was clear. It wasn't about altruism. It was a quest.

Two years earlier, after I'd had a mastectomy, a plastic surgeon fabricated an apparently normal body part to fill my sudden emptiness. The first time we met, he had just returned from his yearly Operation Smile mission to China, where he renovated children's damaged faces. He still wore the aura of his recent experience; I was in a zone of heightened sensibility, on alert and grasping for comfort. What he radiated came from somewhere beyond the usual, and I linked it with where he had just come from.

Because of him, when a local Op Smile clinic was held in Nashville, I helped. The children who came for treatment had somehow slipped through the health-care cracks; their anomalies ranged from webbed fingers, disfiguring port-wine stains and burn scars, to hemangiomas and cleft lips. I was fascinated, not by their alienating differences, but by their course of transfiguration in this newly discovered wonder-world of compensation and resurrection. Without medical training, I could handle logistics, oil the wheels. I held children, sat with their parents through the surgeries; I was a voyeur, but with an urgency. My surgeon let me watch his cleft cases in the operating room, standing on a stool behind him, my hand on his shoulder for balance. I felt the intricate movements of his hands work their way up his arm to where I was holding on. Peering down, I saw him lift those children's sentences of abnormality and felt a fleeting but palpable rush. I had tasted the certainty of possibility.

That was what I wanted more of—to be close to the power of transformation and healing. I signed up for a two-week project in the place that so many of my generation had desperately tried to avoid, or had gone to, only to return permanently altered. Vietnam, a history hole filled with the ghosts of unfinished business, fraught with still-festering sores and old, tender bruises, shimmered with alluring, metaphoric possibilities.

I tried to pack light. Forget the French dictionary, someone told me. "No one will speak that colonial language now." The mission coordinator said to bring scrubs for the OR and modest gifts for my Vietnamese counterparts, whoever they would be. "Bring a fanny pack for your passport, tickets and money, and never take it off." My baggage was full of good intentions, 200 frog finger puppets, some trepidation, a little heavy on the mea culpa. Of course, I wasn't fully prepared.

Reconnaissance

The advance team, 15 of the crew of 36, met at the L.A. airport. It was like a group blind date; we would recognize each other by the smile pins we were supposed to wear. I didn't put mine on. What if it wasn't cool? There were seasoned hands on that flight: surgeons who had been doing this for years, nurses who had taken their two-week vacations and done Kenya, Nicaragua, Romania, Colombia. I was a groupie to their band of common experience. I had no idea what my role would be, but I wanted to be needed.

And I wanted to know these strangers in some essential way. Then, I hoped, I would know a mighty source. If I could capture their experience in words, I would own it. I kept a journal.

Hong Kong to Ho Chi Minh City. Across the aisle is Susan, from L.A., plastic surgery team leader. Her husband, David, a helicopter-door gunner in '69, will help with medical records. This is his first time back to Vietnam; they are holding hands. Valerie has done volunteer anesthesiology in Ecuador. Fred, 73, retired from private practice 10 years ago and does eight volunteer medical trips a year with his wife, Pat, an OR nurse. Jackie, a pediatric intensivist and one of the 30-somethings in the group, has done her homework and shares my sense of incongruity about our destination.

Vietnam, now a frontier tourist destination, is beautiful and flowering, says my Lonely Planet guide. It tells me where to buy the best baguette and to visit the Chu Chi tunnels. Beware of vendors hawking alleged MIA remains. Don't drink the water. Don't climb inside bomb craters. Have a drink at Apocalypse Now. Tet is a time to celebrate. VC and DMZ have changed to BR and NGO.

Our translators are the Viet Kieu, those phantasmal boat people, now citizens of other worlds, sailing back through the sky. All of them are fragments, scattered years ago from secret harbors. Some of them remember last year's mission when immigration officers in Hanoi harassed them, called them traitors, kept them dangling for days. Still, they are coming back.

Next to me, Diep is checking and rechecking her visa. Her father was a South Vietnamese army captain, and her mother worked for the CIA. Their ID cards said they were fishermen when they put out to sea. We have been talking about ghosts, those who died for the wrong reasons, against their karma, without proper rituals. Faceless, nameless hoverers, unattached to any place, she says. Ngoc, a row behind, is a biomedical technician from Orlando who served in the South Vietnamese navy until the day he saw his port city blown up from the ship he was on, which kept going, leaving his wife and children behind. He tells me that the airplane we are now on is his time machine, taking him back to reconnect with his people. More than translation, there will be interpretation.

Can Tho, population 150,000, sits on the lip of a river capillary in the heart of the Mekong Delta. To get there we ride Highway 1, blazing with heat and crawling with life. It is a six-hour bus ride, with two ferry crossings, from what is still called Saigon by almost everyone. My tourist map shows points of interest: pagodas, battle sites, resorts. My own markings on it show where friends have fought and bled and killed. We wait in the sweltering street for our bus to be loaded onto a ferry, engulfed by a tumult of exotic daily activities, children swarming, pushing fly-encrusted snacks in baskets at us. Alice, a recovery-room nurse, 55, blond, dainty and parched, says, "Isn't this wonderful? Do you realize how lucky we are to be here?" It's a far cry, that's for sure.

The hotel is owned by the army. It is grim, with tube lights and heavy cooking smells in the steamy halls. But it has toilet paper and hot water. My roommate, post-op nurse Marja, unloads her gear: antibacterial hand cleaner, biological odor eliminator, 40 bottles of Children's Tylenol, hairdryer and a scented candle. She tells me the children will love the frog finger puppets. It is 12 hours later than it is in Nashville. Inside my mosquito net, I cannot sleep. It isn't Marja's snoring or the splutter of the diesel-powered fishing boats in the canal outside the window, but the din inside my head.

Triage

At 6 a.m. we eat noodle soup with lime and chili while Khai Nguyen, our logistics coordinator from headquarters in Virginia, gives instructions. He hands out copies of the screening-location layout and tells us about Typhoon Linda. Two days ago most of the Delta was flooded, and the provinces targeted for this mission were hit the hardest. We don't know how many children will make it. Next, he gives cultural instructions: Don't touch the tops of the children's heads where their spirits live; don't show anger toward anyone because you will lose face and they will be embarrassed for you.

At 7 a.m. we troop off the bus at a low-slung, crumbling compound wearing our smile buttons, stethoscopes, fanny packs, khakis and Reeboks. We are a team—strong, equipped and totally alien.

We are met by a throbbing crowd of faces, most of them terrible mistakes. Children with no roofs inside their mouths, tongues coming from places where nostrils should be, tusk-like teeth protruding from slabs of gum at the bottom of a nose that didn't happen, vestiges of bifurcated lips. Mesmerized by the profusion of deformity, I am useless.

A friend who heard that I was going to Vietnam to help plastic surgeons repair children's facial disfigurations and burn injuries had said, "Oh, from the war." She'd had a momentary time warp. Those children would, of course, be more than 25 years old now. These children are only the latest ravaged casualties of nature and accident.

Amanda, 25, the child-life specialist from Charleston, is armed with stuffed animals. She expects these barely clothed children to share. They have traveled for hours or days to get here, on foot or by bus, their houses inundated by the typhoon. They share. I am assigned to crowd control, which means keeping it at bay, letting in five at a time to be chosen or rejected for surgery. I use my hands to make futile pushing-away gestures at the surging tide of desperation.

Lucy, clinical coordinator and Navy captain, processed Haitian refugees on the high sea. She says it was the best time of her life. Now she volunteers 75 percent of her time. She pulls tables and chairs into a pattern, musters the local hospital personnel and a translator. Those from the farthest provinces are seen first. Histories and vitals are taken. Surgeons make their evaluations and send the children on through dental, anesthesiology, speech pathology, pediatrics and photos. Photos. I can collate forms and put them in the charts, fill in the date. I can hostess, welcome and guide the mangled flow with directional body language, and look into their eyes.

They are manifestations of heaven and earth. A mother wears wide, black peasant pants and a boxy shirt, holds a conical straw hat, her feet bare. Her 12-year-old daughter wears a black T-shirt that says "Versace Jeans Couture." Jackie is worried about her asthma. I am worried about the rest of her life if she is rejected. Susan and Fred are excited about another girl—the syndromic 16-year-old with lustrous, long black hair, monstrous eye and facial clefts, a tangled mouth. I am having a hard time looking at her and struggling with aversion that I don't want to admit. Her bombed-out communication center, fully exposed, is the aftermath of a capricious rampage. Abandoned, reclusive, estranged, her name is Hai, and she can be fixed.

The surgeons can see just by looking, how to release spirits trapped deep in prisons of distortion, how to repair the shattered gates. Rejected: the boy so anemic his nails were blue, the feverish babies, the asthmatics. Marja does the body weight; Susan does the fate weight.

Larry, the orthodontist, examines a tall, gaunt woman. Her top front teeth, at right angles to her exposed gums, protrude between the two sides of her split upper lip, which is open to the base of her nose. Susan and I watch her as she crosses the room, a graceful specter, blank-eyed, vacant or fear filled. Susan says, "In one hour her whole life can be changed. I want to do it." I look at the chart: Age, 47.

"It's coming so late in life for her," I say, thinking of loneliness.

"Who is that man with her?" Susan asks Ngoc.

"Her brother," he says. "Her husband couldn't come. He had to stay with their five children at home far away." Susan laughs at our assumptions, at our limited understanding. "It was a love marriage," Ngoc says. "But because of poverty she had to go out in public to work. She was always taunted, but the family strength supported her."

"Still," Susan says, "her whole life will be changed."

By afternoon, 120 surgeries are scheduled. There would have been more but for the typhoon.

R & R

The cargo—5,000 pounds of donated technical equipment; every suture, glove, tube, instrument and IV bag needed for the surgeries; all the anesthesia and medications—is held up in customs. Hospital setup is on hold. Don't they want us to do this? All those waiting faces, and we have the morning off. Khai, who is only 25, negotiates with the intractable customs officials. His Vietnamese is fluent, though he grew up in Canada. His job description includes cultural acrobatics, mostly balancing. His memory holds his own family in a small, crowded fishing dinghy, adrift and storm tossed, 16 years ago. He arranges a boat trip down the Mekong River for the team to fill the time.

The banks of the Mekong are clotted with habitation and green, lush growth. We are fighting dehydration and exhaustion and starting to get acquainted. I catch Jackie's eye, knowing she, too, is seeing in black and white: boys who are not there, chest deep, guns raised, wading next to us. I ask Fred about cross-cultural surgery. Is operating on an Asian face different than on a Western one? "Different emphasis on the same thing," he says. "The objective is always symmetry and harmony."

Susan leans forward and holds me with her eyes. "Symmetry, Melissa, not perfection," she says. "We try to make the part commensurate with the whole."

"They need what we have to give them," Fred says, "but differently than we need." I'm not sure what he means. Perhaps, I think, the proportions are different.

We're sipping on straws stuck into the navels of coconuts, sucking on the milk. Pat is telling a story about a project she and Fred were on in the Amazon rain forest. Fred had just finished a boy's lip under local anesthesia, and the boy asked to see his face. No one had a mirror so Pat found a shiny metal trash-can lid and moved it around in front of him till he got a glimpse. Everyone listening to this nods, having heard all the parts she didn't tell. Someone else tells about local nurses in Kenya emptying the suctioning equipment out the back door of the OR into the dirt road. Then it's on to legendary stories of love affairs between teammates that bloomed in the desert, or the jungle, and how they'd only meet on missions. Moving along to Remember Whens, more mutual references, risks taken, crises survived or not. Together, at different times and places. I am adrift in this boat, an audience apart, rapt.

Briefing

Today the team will make presentations to their Vietnamese counterparts at the educational symposium. The hospital classroom is full of surgeons, nurses, anesthesiologists and dentists. The director of the hospital, middle aged, ruddy and rumpled, welcomes us. Ngoc translates and sweats in his white shirt and tie and the 100-degree heat. Overhead fans stir the melting pot. I sit between two Vietnamese women about my age, our shoulders crowded against each other. We smile awkwardly across a vast divide. John, anesthesiology team leader, talks about safety and the problems of using Western medical techniques in countries where resources are less developed. "In the U.S. the doctor looks at the monitor. Here, we must look at the patient."

The women next to me don't speak any English. I take a chance and ask in French, "What is your work?" Lights go on, and French words come out as heavily accented with Vietnamese as mine were with American English. I can almost understand. A few more tries and I know that one is the head nurse and the other a dentist. They ask if I have children, and about what work I will do this week. I try to explain; they smile and nod at me. We dig with primitive tools. Susan shows surgery slides and talks about the psychological effect of disfigurement and the inability to communicate. I smile at these women across a smaller void than before.

Reinforcements

Bravado is in the air. The rest of the team, 21 more, arrived last night. Tonight we have a mandatory group dinner for merging purposes. A bonded team is a better team, according to past experience. John observes, "These are mostly people who are used to being in charge, and now they have to work together." Susan's job is to make controlling their egos seem like fun. There is hilarity and cold Tiger Beer flowing with the platters of rice and shrimp and presentation of the selves.

Carl, a newly arrived plastic surgeon, loudly announces, "I do this for two reasons only: to do challenging plastic surgery and to drink." His cosmetic practice is lucrative, he adds. "Only 10 percent of what I'll do here will be for good-guy points," he says, putting his arms around the nurses on either side of him. So far, I've had "to make a difference" and "pay back" thrown at me as tidbits when I've probed some depths, searching for clues to what makes these people tick, but I can't swallow those sound-bites whole.

I walk back to the hotel after dinner through the dark streets of Can Tho with Court, another plastic surgeon, 48 years old, from New York. We talk about a niche we both came from having to do with straw-bottomed Chianti bottles and war protesting. When I say that the empty bottle was always used as a candleholder and that protesting had been a rite of passage, we connect. Children follow us calling, "Hello, hello, hello," and want to hold our hands. Court says, "The war ripped our generation apart, literally. I was in medical school when my best friend was killed here. I've been coming back on medical missions for years, trying to heal those wounds."

Staging

The cargo was delivered at midnight. Khai, John and Dr. Thong, the Vietnamese head anesthesiologist, carried it to the third floor of the old barren hospital. This morning we are stockpiling supplies by area. Tomorrow is surgery. Anesthesiology unpacks machines, tubes, masks. John, a lanky circulating hawk, tests every function. Here, he says, is what not to do to a child, as he shakes a doll in another anesthesiologist's face. "Would that calm you down?"

A flood in the storeroom soaks the cardboard boxes of IV bags. I move and re-sort them. The post-op area has no cupboards for a pharmacy, so we make some from large cartons and tape. Larry gives toothbrushes to the families who have been cooking and sleeping in the narrow halls, sharing two bathrooms. They have no place else to go. Amanda, her orange hair aflame in the sun, is on the roof with dusky children, blowing bubbles and showing them how to anesthetize themselves with gas masks. The ID bracelets are missing. Recovery needs a fan; there's no air conditioning in there. We pack in cartons of Vietnamese mineral water aptly named La Vie.

Pat and I are doing the ritual checking of the major and minor cleft palate sets: metal boxes of slender, stainless instruments with names like Mosquito Clamp, Two Prong Rake, the Freer Elevator. Carefully, they are swaddled in cloth and sterilized in an autoclave we hope is working. My own instruments, pen and notebook, are cached in a bag in Larry's makeshift lab, where he is setting up to make prosthesis palates, like retainers, for the surgically ineligible.

Children are piled at the barred windows, peering in at us. The stage is set. We pass John's readiness inspection and slip away through the waiting patient families while Hong, the barefoot, pregnant orderly, does a final sterilization.

At dinner Khai says, "Be on the bus at 7 tomorrow morning. We cut at 7:30."

Surgery Day One

The hospital is still, the people quiescent, expectant. A little girl meets me on the stairs and presses something into my hand, smiling with her eyes and part of her mouth. It is rice, wrapped in a banana leaf, bound with string.

Diep and Lucy locate the first patients, line them up with their families on a bench in the hallway, and write names, weights, ages and procedures on their white hospital pajamas. They have been given soap to bathe with, but most of them haven't; there are only two bathrooms and a trickle of water. Diep translates, goes over what will happen, says they shouldn't be afraid. If they are, they don't show it. The five anesthesiologists, their faces still uncovered, come to get the children. Valerie talks to her first patient through Diep as they walk, holding hands, into the OR. A young mother kissing her baby's cleft lip looks up to Craig, who plays with him for a minute before taking him from her reluctant arms. Down the hall, the next on the schedule wait silently.

On the table, Valerie shows her child how to hold the mask to her own face, holds her in her arms and murmurs in her ear as she melts. Consciousness controllers and guardians by trade, the anesthesiologists hold these lives in limbo. "In these little bodies," Valerie says, "things can go bad real fast."

At 7:45 the five tables are filled with sleeping cases. There are two double-table rooms and a single. "This is a brutal surgery," Geoff says, almost apologetically. He will move the lining of the 5-year-old's mouth from where it has mistakenly migrated to the sides of the roof, to where it should be. "We plow it up from the bone with a crude tool. All but one of the vessels that cross over out of the bone into the tissue are severed. Everything at the margin has the capacity to bleed." But fusion of the two released sides will mean internal symmetry. It will mean normal eating, breathing and, maybe, speaking. In the bony corners and at the frontal tip of the roof there will be no stitches holding the repaired tissue in place, only threadlike anchors. And, Geoff says, in two days it will have adhered and healed through self-regeneration.

By 8 our blue scrubs are sweat soaked. The ORs have window air conditioners that clatter in counterpoint to the grinding noise of ancient suction machines and Sting on the tape player. One cauterizing unit for two tables means that Kate, the circulating nurse, has to hook it up and unhook it as it is needed for each patient. She hopes they won't need it at the same time.

Now, Valerie and Craig carry their drugged children, with nurses holding the IV bags aloft like victory flags, to recovery. They stay, watching, while Alice and Lisa do vitals, wipe off the blood, check the breathing. At this way station, hovering consciousness is monitored by sight and touch. Lisa is holding a baby with one arm and the baby's IV bag with the other hand. "Melissa, get me some tape. This needle is coming out." I don't know where the tape is. When I find it, I can't rip a piece off. That's all she needs, a piece of torn tape. My fingers are swollen from the heat and won't manipulate. I don't have the right angle on the rip. Lisa is looking at me, sweat beads on her lip. "OK, hold the bag, I'll get it," she says.

Alice is partly lying on top of a thrashing child, trying to hold the thermometer in his armpit. She asks me to help her. I don't know what to do, but she shows me how to hold his arm, where to put my body weight. I think *What if this were my child*, and he begins to calm. Alice's face is close to mine. As we release our grip, she says, "These trips are how I mainline to what is meaningful to me about what I do; I can go directly to the art part of nursing. No monitoring crutches between me and the patient, just basic skills, hands-on care and feeling."

Jackie is a sentinel in her baseball cap, her starched white coat brilliant against her glistening, dark-brown skin, a bright toy attached to her stethoscope. She stalks trouble in recovery: vomiting, fever, bleeding palates. Geoff comes in between surgeries to look at his 5-year-old, who is seeping ceaselessly. The tannic acid in a wet tea bag is supposed to constrict vessels, and one has been pressed inside the child's mouth, the string and Lipton label trailing from his swollen lips. Geoff takes it out and puts his finger inside with a wad of Surgicel, putting pressure on the palate "until I feel it seat," he says. "Sometimes you have to safeguard your surgery." Mike, who assisted on this child, slides his finger in over Geoff's, and they wait together until Mike has the feel of the pressure and can take over. Twenty minutes later, when I bring some charts, he still stands there, bent over, concentrating.

"This one's ready for post-op. David, can you get him?" David, the door gunner, puts down his camcorder and turns around. When was the last time he carried a Vietnamese child? This is a large one, and he's not sure where to put his hands. A Vietnamese nurse shows him how to pick the boy up while she untangles the tubes. I open the door and am met by a surge of expressionless parents, wanting their children. What can David be thinking? He moves in a dreamer's slow motion down the hall to post-op, his face flooded with radiance, the child's father following at a distance.

There, each straw-mat-covered bed holds two recovering children and two parents sharing space meant for one. Neatly folded into their tight spaces, water bottles, food vessels and cooking utensils arranged around them, they exude distress. No translators are here now to explain that the long black threads coming from their children's mouths, taped to their cheeks, are tongue stitches for emergency airway clearance. That the moaning and lethargy are normal. That the swelling will get worse before it gets better. I am standing in the middle of the throng, holding a small yellow basin filled with cotton swabs, waiting for someone to need one. Jackie is in here assessing and catches me in her sweep. "How are you doing?" she asks, as if I am her patient.

"I'm not doing anything," I say, with a minor but discernible tremor.

As if I am her child, she puts her arm around me and says, "Every touch, every word, every look is doing." And she leaves me standing here.

Marja says that when the children were put on pre-op "nothing by mouth" orders, the parents stopped eating and drinking, as well. Now they are exhausted and dehydrated, fanning their fragile children, whose identities have been tampered with. She asks me to find a translator so she can talk to the parents; she cannot decipher their blank faces. "In Kenya they were into jubilation at this point," she says. Here, only their pleading eyes speak. Thanh, a post-op nurse from Virginia, spent four nights alone, at age 17, on a small boat crammed with 63 strangers. When it beached on a wild island near Malaysia, everyone foraged, everyone shared. She tells us that the parents are suffering because their children are suffering.

An old woman beckons to me and points at the black stitches in her sleeping child's lip. I squat next to the bed and touch the child's forehead, as if I have a right. The skin is smooth and cool. When I look up I see that the woman is waiting for me and that the expression on my face is mirrored in hers; she smiles back at me, toothlessly.

Thanh tells me that this woman is the child's neighbor. Her grandmother, with whom she has lived since her parents abandoned her, is blind and couldn't make the five-hour bus trip, the two days walking. "There is a word in Vietnamese, *tôt*, that means good person, someone who has the capacity for caring, for doing good," Thanh tells me.

"Ask her why she did this for the child," I say.

But Thanh shakes her head and says, "If you claim your good deeds, then they don't count. The act in itself is enough."

Later, Mike comes into the lunchroom, ebullient. The bleeder had fallen asleep biting down on his finger. "He felt comfortable with me taking care of him—that's the greatest feeling—and when I took my finger out and looked inside with a flashlight, it was pink and clean and gorgeous."

Retreat

The local staff will take the all-night shift. We are on the hotel roof in the moonlight drinking Tiger Beer and tightening the invisible thread holding us together. Carl has ordered in dinner for everyone. Six people in cycle cabs deliver and serve us the fragrant, eight-course meal. The child-size plastic chairs we have brought up from the hotel's waterfront café are tight fits. When we stand up to form a loose circle, they are stuck to us.

Twenty-five surgeries today. Some of us have showered; some are just coming in. Valerie is spent and upset. "It was a really good day, but my last case was a 3-year-old who started calm but at the last minute went ballistic with fear." No slack for her, no margins. Her mission is to mitigate pain, and fear is pain.

Geoff, who is tall and broad, is cramped in the little chair. His cases today were one lip, three palates and a combo. "I forgot how exhausting the palates are," he says. "You have to hunch, crane, contort. I'm completely steamrollered." Last year Geoff did this in China.

"Why do you really do this?" I ask between bites, expecting the standard gloss.

"Everyone is born with a gift that must be recognized and shared," he says, lighting up. "Whatever it is." Whatever? Everyone? He has obviously thought about this before; I want to hear more, but he looks so tired.

Craig, young, blond and single, says, "My friends think I'm crazy to give up two weeks' salary and work in these conditions. But this is what I went into medicine for—pure experience. I don't have to worry about billing, mergers or being sued. Just have to do my best and take care, and I make an impact on someone's life."

Geoff continues, "Working on the human life ups the ante. There is connection through the recipient of our service at the time of their need, and we need to be connected."

Court turns to me and lays his hand on the side of my face. "You have beautiful bone structure." I freeze. "Fat in the right places," he says as he moves his long fingers across my cheek. Beneath my skin lies a skeletal cage of bird-bones, crushable. "Well preserved for your age."

"I exercise," I say, suddenly fragile and exposed.

"Nothing to do with it; it's genetic." So, roll of the dice, luck of the draw. I long to press my forehead into his palm; instead, I move away. His gesture, deeply personal and impersonal, is not what I expected. This isn't supposed to be about me. Or is it?

I corner John before he goes to bed. Every morning before breakfast, when he jogs along the canals, people washing their clothes and preparing their breakfasts wave and greet him. He's drinking La Vie and rubbing his eyes, but he leans toward me with attention. "I had a savage childhood," he says, unwrapping himself like a gift. "Raised in a boys' home, an orphanage. I guess I do this to reconcile my life, to reinforce to myself that I'm capable of good. Having a good heart means having the capacity for caring. I do good for others so I'll feel good about myself."

Fred is a toucher. He and Pat stop to say good night on their way to bed. "Keep asking those questions," he says, putting his arm around me. He is white haired, rugged and very handsome. How did he know what I've been asking? I haven't gotten to him yet. "We're all part of the survival mechanism, aren't we?" he says. "When we do good work as an expression of our inner being, we help the cosmic wheel to turn. The Bhagavad Gita says that work is sacred and pure when it is done with no desire for reward. What we're doing here provides necessary goods and services, but it also helps to liberate us from our egocentricity." He and Pat both hug me and go to bed.

Small pockets of intimacy are forming in the shadows as the dinner is cleared away. Legs propped in one another's laps, backrubs in a circle, low-voiced confessions of divorce, psychoanalysts, disappearing fathers, alcoholic mothers, fractured childhoods, parental pride, marriage advice, successes, dreams. Confidences. Family photos are passed around, offerings of clues to another self. The darker it becomes, the closer we come together. Grown-ups at a slumber party trade visceral revelations in the dark.

Marja, Dominique and Jackie arrange to take turns checking in all night at the hospital, just to make sure.

Surgery Day Two

Dr. Thong bows to me at the post-op door. "*Bonjour, Madame.*" The Vietnamese nurses ripple in to get the room ready for morning rounds. They brush against me, trailing their arms around my shoulders and one another's, like fresh breezes. The head nurse gives me a piece of paper with her name on it. She is Xuan, which means spring in Vietnamese. I tell her mine, honeybee, in Greek. Somehow, through these words, we are related. She tells me in heavily accented French that the ward was quiet all night. This morning the children are sitting up, drinking, eating soup. They are ready to go home. Mike's bleeder has a fever and has to stay. His mother and father are on the bed with him, nesting. Thanh tells me, "That child's mother wants to talk to you."

"The water was waist high in our house when we left," she tells me through Thanh as I settle in beside them. "Without the typhoon it would have taken us only 12 hours to get here. We are rice farmers. Our ancestors did not have this face problem. We were sad when he was born like that." I know about the clefted babies preserved in bottles at the War Remnants Museum in Saigon and the sign on them that says: "The Result of Agent Orange."

"Why do you believe this happened to your child?" I ask.

"The fault is in my past life. I did something very bad."

"And why do you think that he has been fixed, now?"

"Because in this life, I have been very good. And I am lucky." She leans toward me and puts her hand on mine. "I wish that you could come to my house. I wish that we could talk together, about many things. I can never repay what you have done." I wish I had done the surgery, but I am her conduit to the team. And I am the one sitting here, holding hands with her. I would give anything to go home with her, to sit by her cooking fire, to see the neighbors come acknowledge the lifting of her shame. To see this seemingly random redemption through to the end.

For two hours Court has been rearranging Hai's face and teaching new techniques to visiting surgeons from Saigon. I could be helping Amanda with the toys and games or sorting folders with Diep. But I can't seem to leave the foot of this table. Valerie tells how Hai ran into the OR, pulled the mask to her face and inhaled with all her might. Now her slender feet are turned up and outward; her flat stomach moves almost imperceptibly with breath. Valerie's eyes move in a steady pattern between her, the minimal machines and gauges, the tubes and wires. She doesn't mention that Hai had asked to keep her bra on, dingy cotton, now loose over her small, sleeping breasts.

A crowd gathers around her head, each American with a Vietnamese counterpart. Two anesthesiologists, two surgeons, two nurses. Pat offers to make room for me if I don't touch anything. I can hardly breathe behind my mask; the paper shower cap holds the sweat in place. I move in closer, close enough to see that Hai has been dismantled. Like small red flags, splayed, the flaps of her face are inside out. Court is tailoring without a pattern and explaining his decisions as he makes them. Long silences are cut by bursts of words heavy with exertion. Fred comes over from the other table in the room to look, but I cannot anymore. I feel a scream coming on, my mind groping in panic for the hand brake. Ever the one trying to put together things gone asunder, what can I do in the face of this total deconstruction? Still, I cannot leave the foot of the table.

"That's it," Court says and steps back. Now I can see what he has done. "In the U.S. it would be better," he says. "We would have taken a flap from her back to fill out her cheeks, and the lip needs a touch-up later. But this is pretty good." In fact, even with black railroad-track stitches running the lengths of her cheeks and around her mouth, even with her eyes temporarily sewn shut, she is almost beautiful. Court pulls off his mask and cap. He is flushed and bathed in sweat as he tells Mike, "It doesn't get better than that. The essence of plastic surgery is creativity. You can't find a textbook that tells you how to do that operation; there's no recipe. You have your concepts of tissue movement, so you put them together with a plan for a specific patient. Then, things change as you do it. Things you don't expect come up. This goes beyond technicianship, and when you get a good result it is absolutely thrilling. It's why I do plastic surgery." Unconsciously, he is stroking Hai's arm with his bare, ungloved hand.

Amanda has collected all the handmade dolls without faces that were sent in the cargo and given out this morning. Ladies at auxiliary meetings somewhere in the States made them, chatting over tea and cookies about how much fun it would be for the little Vietnamese children to draw on the faces. "These are a big mistake here," Amanda says. "When these people see no faces, they see ghosts." No face, no identity.

We draw on the faces and return them to the children.

Hump Day

There is a square in the center of the town, and in its early-morning gardens the people gather like dew to perform Tai Chi. A conductorless ensemble, each is his own instrument. Ngoc, merged in their daily midst, flowing in their current, is dawn dancing for the restoration of consonance.

I am going to interview the hospital director. Juliette, born Quang Tri, who married an American civil engineer in 1970, will translate. While we wait for Dr. Huan to emerge from his afternoon nap on the cot behind a screen in his office, she says, "All these years I could not communicate with my people. Now I can help them. Doing good deeds during my life means that my children and grandchildren will be blessed in future lives."

Dr. Huan's many Vietnamese words go into Juliette and come out of her in condensed English. He grew up near Da Nang and studied medicine in Hanoi. He is 50 years old; we are of the same generation. Suddenly, he looks at me directly and says, in French, "During the American War, I worked with a medical team in the jungle." Now there is no filter; we are eye to penetrating eye. He says, "I was with the National Liberation."

Juliette, close to me, breathes, "VC." The hairs on my arms stand at attention; blood presses behind my eardrums.

He and his superiors have always had the same aim, he says: unification, which has allowed his country to receive help from worldwide humanitarian organizations. He is happy to have us in Can Tho because of the skills we bring and the numbers we help. But, he says, "Most important is the friendship. This does not depend on who gives what, or how much, but on the person who brings good things." Is he for real?

I write in my notes: "I am in the Mekong Delta speaking French with the Viet Cong." In case I wake up, I want a record.

Record keeping is, in fact, now part of my job description. Khai has asked me to keep a daily journal for him to use in writing his final report. As resident errand-runner and odd-jobber, I circulate through the whole project freely, like a roving camera, observing and documenting. Of course, the mental pictures I take and develop are filtered through the lens of myself.

The 47-year-old woman whose life Susan wanted to change is on her table. We figure that she would have been 20 when David was here before, when Dr. Huan was in the jungle. Larry has extracted her front teeth. Susan says, "You know, during the war, American surgeons would pull cleft kids out of the paddies and fix them when things were slow." *Like fishing*, I think, as Susan ties off her knots on this belated catch.

I don't remember these four teen-age girls, perched together on a bed in post-op, warily watching me dip a cotton swab in peroxide solution. They don't know that I am not a nurse or that when I clean their wounds, it will not hurt. So close to them I feel their body heat, so lightly I pass the swab across the scabs. The way their black hair falls in their faces, I want to smooth it back. They have been here for a week, being processed, living meagerly. Now, I want to touch them, but they are ready to leave with their new faces, their turgid lips tied up with stitches.

There are monks in the halls, bare armed, shaven headed, saffron robed. Silent. They wait for Valerie. Last night she went to their pagoda with Amanda, Craig and Dominique for services and chanting. They singled her out to read an X-ray, the inside of one of the monks, shadows and light of a foreign land better understood by this gentle foreigner. That they came, trusting, bestows blessing. When they are gone, the scent of incense lingers where they were.

It is 9:15 at night, and two tables are still working, one of them Fred's. When the power fails he is deep into an operation. Suddenly, it is dark and silent. Pat reaches up and switches on the headlight strapped to his head. Fred has been around the block; he doesn't waver for a second.

Surgery as Metaphor

There is a congregation around Susan's table, all masked. She and Court, the protester, have been sharing technique; he is going to watch her next case. Dr. Thong, South Vietnamese, is intubating the 6-month-old baby asleep in front of us. Ngoc, Viet Kieu, checks the electrical connections. David, veteran, is videotaping from a height at the foot of the table. The Viet Cong director stands behind Susan at the head. This gathering is a remarkable confluence. Susan says, "Plastic surgery puts the missing pieces into a puzzle."

She draws a coded map along the crest of the cleft lip. Now she follows the trail of blue dots with a knife and then with a scissors. "You have to take it all apart," she says, "so you can put it back together the way it should be." Beyond skin, she goes down to the deepest levels, revealing infantile, raw meat. She snips tiny scraps of tissue from either side, placing the moist rubies on the sterile blue sheets. "This buildup of scar-like tissue is characteristic of the cleft condition and has to be removed, for release and mobility. I take it out, make fresh surfaces, and now, start stitching. First, the underlying muscle. Then, the part that shows."

A simple thing, this fissure fusion, but not easy. Susan tugs gently on the baby's skin with suture in one hand and tiny tweezers in the other, aligning, pressing it together like a little pie crust. His nose and mouth are now symmetrical, unified by this collective karma correction. Just then, the thread pulls up tight, and in an infinitesimal moment of suspended time, there is closure.

Surgery Day Five

The director is in when I go calling, alone. "*Monsieur*," I say, "*La vie est très compliquée*," as I hand him the modest gift I have brought for my unknown counterpart. Suddenly, I have no words in any language. If he looks in my eyes, he will see unexpected tears. "*C'était une expérience très unique, pour moi. Merci*," I say. He does look into my eyes, bows and smiles.

John flits from table to table, dancing down the hall to Reggae music between the operating rooms. He is celebrating the success of the project's safety standards on this last day of surgery. Xuan and I share family photos and exchange addresses. In recovery, Lisa and Alice change the dressing on a skin graft. They ask me to make sure the 14-year-old boy who has just been brought in doesn't fall out of bed.

He is agitated. There are no translators nearby. Semi-awake, his free arm is up in the air waving around; he moans. I stand next to him; he tries to tell me something. Wide-eyed, he reaches toward me. I take his dry, rough hand in mine, and he pulls me to him so that I am leaning over him, my hand now under his, on his chest. He holds me. His breathing slows; he is peaceful, and so am I. He takes the mirror I give him and looks at himself for a long time. I can't tell him that the swelling is temporary, that the stitches will disappear. He can't tell me

55

anything, but he has tears in his eyes. He gives a thumbs-up and falls asleep smiling, his hand still gripping mine. Engulfed, I am awash.

Jackie watches me from a corner, her brimming eyes beaming into mine. She, too, has been carried away in this rush; we have lost ourselves together at the point of convergence. Here it is, the last day, and I am just getting started. If only I could plunge like this and stay immersed indefinitely.

Rounds

A few patients remain to be discharged. All the parents want their children looked at and are anxious to leave. I take dictated notes from Geoff who, with Mike and Thanh, are responsible for this last day of post-op. Patient No. 124, large clot extracted from both lateral troughs, no active bleeding, institute rinses; No. 113, nasal airway collapse in this syndromic infant, possible apnea, repair looks excellent, hold one additional day to evaluate airway; No. 079, lip repair, no infection, adequate oral intake, home today with instructions. Thanh translates between Geoff, the parents and the Vietnamese staff and portions out liquid Tylenol into zipper-lock bags for the families to take with them.

I have been watching Mike as he looks inside mouths with his penlight to check the palates. On the end of the tiny flashlight is a green frog finger puppet. "Look at this," he says to me. He shines the beam inside the child's mouth, which is covered with a thick, white coating. "That's fibrin, a protein. It's the body's way of sealing itself off when there's injury. The protective fibrous network it forms helps the body to heal." What I see is divine fabric, a second skin on every surface. When it is gone, only the scar of the reconstructed central fusion line will remain. This self-healing is, to me, a cause for celebration. Mike gives the child the frog, which, it turns out, symbolizes wisdom and kindness in Vietnam.

No. 082, Hai. It is time to cut the stitches holding her eyelids shut. Geoff asks me to put soaking, wet cotton pads on them to loosen the dried crust before he starts. For days she has been locked inside her head alone, with the windows shuttered. Now she begins to tremble.

I hold Hai's hands as Geoff snips the eyelid threads. With each snip she flinches and tries to fend him off. When he has finished she struggles to open her swollen eyes to the coaxing of the Vietnamese nurses who have gathered. The first reflection she has of herself, as she squints against the light, is in their eager faces. Then, she sees herself in the small pocket mirror one of them offers. Her young uncle, who has been taking care of her, squats on the end of her cot. He tells us that she has lived with him for 10 years, since her parents abandoned her. She takes care of his children, who love her, does the cooking and cleaning, and never leaves the house. Why has he accepted her? I ask. "Because she is my niece; it's only normal." And he begins to weep.

Hai has been made symmetrical, harmonious, pleasing on the outside. But this kind of deliverance has another side, another kind of aftermath. Her internal armor, her fortifications, her mask are still in place. The fibrous network holding her together is her own self's ability to regenerate. This is beyond appearance. It will be months before these external scars fade and she moves on. Now, she doesn't know who she is. No wonder she is crying.

I should have known this. Geoff, whose plastic surgery practice is 80 percent reconstructive and 20 percent cosmetic, knows about parents who need days to re-bond with children whose anomalies have been corrected and about patients who face identity complications after a nose job. He doesn't even have the language with which to speak to this teen-ager in his simple, clear way. She won't open her eyes again. Tears stream from their corners. The bundle of clothes under her head is soaked. I look up at Geoff's unreadable face. I want him to be in charge here, but he is not. He has not relinquished control; he never had it.

My thoughts veer away, touching my reconstructed right breast, an understudy for deformity, hidden beneath my clothes. I remember the follow-up to my surgery, which involved refinement of shape and creation of an artificial nipple. I had opted for local anesthesia because I wanted to be there, I thought, to experience part of my own restoration. But this was a ruse. After all, not long ago my surgeon had had his hands deep under my skin, burrowing in fleshly manipulation. This time I was trying to get inside him as he crafted an intimate anatomical body part from a harvested graft. I strained to see, from my restricted position, through his glasses. In profile, I saw his eyes, amber, translucent, steady, but not what they saw. I had wanted more than to be done to, but my conscious presence had been a delusion of superintendence.

Geoff, standing here over Hai's bed, is a finely honed instrument, a corporeal strategist in this battle, having done here in Vietnam what he does well and what gives him satisfaction in Fort Wayne. No more, no less. The real power, I am beginning to see, must be intrinsically the patient's. As for control, no one seems to have it.

When the parents were evaluated, days that seem like eons ago, John talked to me about the fluid dynamic that changes with each mission and determines who gets treated and in what order. A combination of variables falls into place: who the surgeons are, what they are strong in, how many patients show up, what capacity the hospital and local staff have for extended care, how healthy the patient is on the day of the screening. He hadn't mentioned typhoons, good neighbors, uncles, decision-making VC directors. And what about the pull of the homeland, war wounds, inarticulated desire, past lives, grace.

What an orchestration to arrive at this crescendo. I have been asking *why* when I should have been asking *how* we all got here: via serendipity and consequential choices made at every crossroad. Here I sit with this survivor, both of us working on second chances that came without guarantees. In fact, all of us, by whichever circuitous, biographical route we took to get here, are hanging by a common thread. So what alchemic incantation can we conjure up to make it strong? *Solve et Coagula*: dissolve and reconstitute, transformation through breakdown, chaos at the critical juncture between changing states. Then, together, we can use the gold to spin a web in time and space, to catch each other, if we are lucky.

Hai is discharged. I cannot bear to watch her leave.

Disengagement

The hospital has been emptied again, the cargo packed up, shipped off. We left behind whatever supplies we could, and something else. On our way out the door we were stopped by a woman carrying a small child with a bilateral cleft lip. Her own face was frozen in panic. She had come too late. The child was dirty and exhausted; they had been traveling for three days. Dr. Thong, who was seeing us off, went to find the Vietnamese surgeons who had worked with us. He returned to say that the surgery would be done when anesthesia equipment could be borrowed. The surgeons had learned new techniques and were ready for this child.

I have photos in my camera of Xuan and me at the farewell banquet, our arms around each other, smiling into the distance. We took turns serving each other from the communal bowls, turning our chop-sticks over and using the clean ends to choose choice morsels for each other, lotus root salad and morning glory stems. Neither of us would eat till the other had been served.

There were speeches after dinner. Ngoc translated as the governor of the province thanked us. "You have demonstrated in actions the words of the U.S. ambassador, who has said that the U.S. wants to build a bridge of friendship between our countries."

Khai, holding the microphone, told the story his mother told him as a child in Vietnam, the one that carried the warning: Be careful, or the monsoon winds will carry you away. "It wasn't the wind that car-ried me away from Vietnam; it was the war," he said to this conflated group. "I was a child of circumstance, just as the children we helped here are. For me, this was more than a humanitarian mission. It was a journey of self-discovery, of finding who I am and why I am the way I am." Alice and I looked at each other across the table, on guard for Khai, who had thrown off his camouflage.

On departure morning the team gathered at the waterfront for photos, in groups of specialty: surgeons, nurses, anesthesiologists. Finally I knew where I belonged: support staff, along with child-life, speech pathology and translators. Of course. Support.

At the Saigon airport I looked at the departure board: Nha Trang, Pleiku, Hanoi. As if those were normal destinations. Stretched to my limit of absorption and inextricably entwined, I left Vietnam and came down from the supramundane.

Correspondents

Back in the world, I long to continue conversations within our mutual context and aim missives at my teammates' fading, receding forms. There is a flurry of communication: season's greetings, photos, lasting impressions. Between the lines I write to stay in touch are deeper meanings, tying things together in myself. Before, I had only tasted the potential of this experience. Now I have gorged myself. Why am I still hungry?

Geoff writes to me, "My life changes directions with these trips. I return valuing material things less and human spirit more. My family and community become higher priorities. I experience a more fun-damental self."

I write back, "How can we know so much about each other while knowing almost nothing about the details of each other's lives? What kind of car do you drive? When is your birthday? Does it even matter?" He sends me his journal of our trip. Our common experience, I see, is a Roshamon—changing, depending on the angle it is seen from. So much for capturing and owning.

On the phone, Court says, "This trip was really good for me; it was purely humanitarian. I saw, finally, that the war is over. My political motivations are jetsam now. Maybe it's time for me to move on."

"It's difficult to explain to my wife about the intensity of emotions on that trip," Carl e-mails. "Simplicity, beauty and love all intermeshed with passion, honesty and trust. I'm less comfortable doing a cleft palate than a facelift, but I was more calm there than back here. It's especially about the trust in each other that we had there." Is this the same guy?

Amanda tells me that she crossed boundaries she hadn't known existed. "I went through their eyes, into their culture, into their lives. They touched me. We touched each other." Her voice drops to a whisper. "It was like being in love."

Fred writes in a surprisingly feathery penmanship, "If work is an expression of love, it does not ask why, for love has no why. My definition of love is quite simple: Love is the Experience of Connectedness." Who wouldn't want more of that?

I didn't know, beforehand, what healing hinged on this multifaceted expression of work. When people ask me now about my recent "adventure," I sometimes say, obscurely, "Well, you only live once. Maybe." But the truth is that one high led to another, one longing to another. This affair is of the mind and the heart, anointed with balm, suffused with addictive elixir, full to overflowing. It seeps through its encapsulating membrane and spreads in rivulets, transforming my internal landscape. I went to Vietnam, was blown away, consumed, and returned permanently altered.

Melissa Bloch writes nonfiction and fiction. She lives in Nashville and is currently at work on a novel set in the south of France.

White Girl in Harlem

Jennifer Jeanne Patterson

Shortly after I arrived in New York City, living a few blocks from Harlem as a graduate student at Columbia University, I stopped wanting to leave my apartment. I started to think something was out there waiting for me. I didn't know what it was. As soon as I left my building, I felt my fear. Like it was taped to my ear. I could feel it, but I couldn't see it. Nor could I describe it. Or understand it. It was a vague fear—all I knew was that I was going to get hurt, but I didn't know how or why I felt that way. At first I thought I'd be hurt on the subway. That somebody would push me onto the tracks, and I'd get run over by a train or electrocuted, so I began to stand away from the tracks. Later I began to think that my train would fall off the tracks. Whenever my train car jerked or lights flashed beneath it, I was sure a car in front of me had fallen off the tracks, and it was only a matter of time before my car went careening into it. I would brace myself, holding onto the pole. I knew I was being ridiculous but couldn't help it. Something was going to happen to me; I just knew it.

I began to fear that somebody, anybody, would attack me on the street. Attack me in a way from which I would never recover. Then my fear began to take shape through a premonition. He came to me in my dreams at first, a black man coming to ask me to pay for his suffering. He stabbed me with knives, silver blades flickering before me. He stabbed my sisters, too. I watched as he sliced skin from their faces. I felt his hate for me. To him I did not exist; he felt nothing when that knife went into me. He didn't care when I screamed because it didn't relieve him of any of his pain. His pain still went on and on; I could see it in his eyes. His hate. His indifference. What scared me the most was that he saw right through me. He saw everything in me but didn't care about any of it. He thought I felt nothing, as I had felt none of what life had dealt him. So he stabbed me to make me feel it, but by then it was too late; all I could feel was fear—fear of him.

Afraid to sleep, I left all the lights on in my apartment, but as soon as I closed my eyes, the man appeared. Every day I grew more exhausted from not being able to sleep.

Soon I started to believe he was real and that he was telling me about his arrival by coming to me through my dreams. Even my building, which had double doors, wasn't secure enough, so I started pushing my dresser up against the door at night, should he get past the guards downstairs. Then one night I thought I saw him enter my room through the window when I had risen from sleep to a semi-conscious state. When I saw him come through the window, all I could do was lie in my bed, immobilized by fear, paralyzed, and watch him. I tried to make myself get up and run to the door, but my legs wouldn't move. I tried rubbing my eyes, but he stayed. At last he left. I woke then and tried to lock my window, but it was already locked, and so I moved my dresser, as it had been blocking my exit. It was ridiculous to think he could climb the flat, brick surface of the building, but I couldn't help myself. I was that sure he was coming.

For the time being, though, he could only get to me through my dreams. I tried to find ways to trick him out of my sleep. I tried sleeping behind my bed, thinking if he did come into my room, he wouldn't find me. I left my blankets and pillows on my bed so it'd appear I just hadn't come home for the night. He still came every night. "This is just a dream!" I heard myself yell as I saw him come in through the window, but I didn't believe it was a dream. I saw him too clearly; I just knew he was real.

It wasn't until my mother came to visit that I started to believe I was going crazy. I hadn't told my mother about my fear. I didn't want to; I knew she wouldn't understand. She would dismiss it, attribute it to stress, but it was more than that. It was taking over my life. I couldn't walk to school without thinking about it; it stopped me from going to class. At night before going to bed, I made sure the door and window were locked, and if I had to go to the bathroom, I tried desperately to hold it in. I didn't want to unlock my door, especially not at night. He could be waiting in the dormitory showers.

I didn't think he'd come the night my mother was there. Before bed I thought to myself, "Tonight, at least, he'll leave me alone. Tonight I can sleep." I prepared for his visit, anyway, by locking everything up. I put on my pajamas and got into bed. To avoid my mother's suspicion, I turned off the lights before lying down beside her and then quickly falling asleep.

I saw him come through the window, but I didn't wake my mother up. I thought he would go away. But he didn't; he just stood there in the corner of the room looking at us both. It was more than I could take.

"He's here!" I hollered. "He's in the room!" I jumped from bed and turned on the light, and he was still there. He was still there! He was standing by the radiator, looking sheepish. He had on green shorts.

"My God, Jennifer," my mother said in disbelief, first blocking her eyes because of the light but then opening them wide to try to see what I saw. "There's nobody here."

But there was, there was! I pointed to him, but in the light he swirled around, broke into bits of dust and disappeared. I had to shake my head to try to get sense back into it. I started to cry.

"It's okay, it's okay," my mother said, bewildered. "Sometimes I have bad dreams, too." But it wasn't a bad dream; it was so much more than that. Didn't she see him? He had been there!

I knew he hadn't. I was convinced I was going crazy.

I was afraid of the beggars on the street, the ones who smelled of urine-soaked clothes and looked as if life had been sucked out of them through their eyes. I hated the way they forced me to look at them by shaking their Styrofoam cups in my face, setting themselves up like tollbooths on Broadway, their jingling coins clanging like cymbals behind my ears. As if to ask, *Have you really done your share?* And when I passed, I knew what they were thinking: *Hey, hey you, you think you got problems? Well, you can disappear—or assimilate, isn't that the fancy word you use?—anytime you want. You think you got problems? You should try my life.* I wanted to yell back at them, *I'm not one of them! Don't you get it?!* But I knew they wouldn't. Because I had already begun to morph.

I worried a beggar would stab me one day for not putting a quarter in his cup. That all that had dried up within him would turn into a terrible blaze one day. I thought I saw him one day, that man who kept coming through my window; I thought I saw him in a black man who came toward me on the street. I could tell he was out of his mind on drugs; he zigzagged down the sidewalk, and right when I was ready to cross, he addressed me in an unnaturally high-pitched voice, "Can I eat your pussy? Can I eat it on a string?" I had to laugh because it was all so surreal, but I stepped out into the street, less afraid of the cars zooming past than of him.

I tried to think where my fear came from. I thought if I could intellectualize it, I could get over it. As I was growing up in a small town in upstate New York, my house had been a block over from the projects, which were predominantly black. I never hung out there. In fact my parents had forbidden us from hanging out with anybody who lived there, black or white. "Animals," my parents had said, after hearing a story from a white neighbor about how a black girl living in the projects had bitten off part of the skin of another. "Animals and trash."

My father, a blue-collar city worker, seemed to fear that most: that one of those black men would blemish the skin of his white daughters. He'd call us inside whenever the black boys tried to talk to us. Sometimes we'd smile back at them when my father wasn't looking; we knew it would infuriate him. But we generally obeyed him, because it was easier to do that than to disobey him.

When he found out one of my friends was black, he forbade me from seeing him but wouldn't give a reason why. "His house is nicer than ours!" I screamed because it was the only thing I could think to say to hurt him, but he didn't respond. He just shook his head and went on watching his TV show.

"Your father's not racist," my mother said when I accused him of being so. "It's just... well, you have to understand what he'd go through..." By that she meant what his co-workers would say. What our neighbors would say. When I got angry with her for saying that, she took a different approach. "It's like the baby bird that falls from its nest. Once the mother bird smells human hands on it, she won't want to touch it." I didn't even want to think about what that analogy meant.

But I was afraid. One night our neighbors were robbed. My younger sister had woken me during the night to say she had heard a snipping sound. I had laughed at her, told her it was a dream and sent her back to bed. The next morning I held her hand as we stood in the driveway watching my father peel back the window screen of our neighbors' home, which had been snipped in two. "Here's where he got in," my father said.

I knew it was just a matter of time before our house was hit.

Our high school had a tracking system under which you took classes according to ability. In my four years of high school, I remember having only two black people in my class. When walking through the school halls, I sometimes peered into one of the basic classes, and it seemed most of the faces that looked back at me were black.

Because of where I lived, I was one of few white people on my bus. I hated taking the bus. When I got on, the black girls would make it clear they did not want to sit with me. "Uh-uh," they'd say, one after another, placing their book bags next to them or moving over so I'd have to climb over them to get a window seat. I didn't fight with them. I would rather have stood, though I knew the bus driver would never allow that. Although it seemed I knew most of the kids at school, at least by sight, there was only one person I ever recognized on the bus. Her name was Kim, a white girl who played on my basketball team and lived a few blocks from me. Usually I sat with her.

The bus dropped us off on one side of a walking bridge, and I lived on the other side of it. Kim and I would walk a few blocks together, and then we would part; I would cross the bridge alone. Usually I'd try to hold Kim up by asking her questions until the black girls crossed the bridge. I didn't want to be on the bridge with them. I wasn't afraid of the black girls I knew from school or basketball, only those I didn't know. A few times after accidentally bumping into one of them in the hallway, I was whapped on the head with a notebook.

One day Kim had to hurry home. I tried to keep her for as long as I could by asking her questions, but it wasn't long enough. I'd have to cross the bridge with the black girls. In fact, I'd have to walk ahead of them. As I started across the bridge, I tried to think of other things to keep my mind distracted. I peered over the edge at the shallow creek below. There was so much garbage down there. I was lost in thought when I heard the girls call to me from a few steps behind.

"Hey, Blondie!"

"Blondie!"

"Oh, Blondie!"

I knew they were talking to me—I was the only other person on the bridge—but I ignored them. I didn't turn around because I didn't want them to see my fear. All I could think to do was to continue walking at the same pace.

"Hey, Blondie!" one of the girls screamed, more belligerently. Feeling I had no choice, I finally turned. My eyes, which never settled on them in the school hallway, now rested on them with fear. My fear ignited them; it empowered them; it angered them. One girl grabbed a handful of my hair and pushed me down on the bridge until I was a supplicant before them. I could smell urine on the concrete. "We hate blondes," the girl said, and the others laughed. I wanted to scream, *What do you want from me? How can I make anything different?* but instead I got up, wiped myself off and continued home.

I could hear their voices as they walked off toward the projects. Once I was on my block, I felt safe. They wouldn't follow me home. That I knew. After walking through the front door of my house, I collapsed in a heap on the kitchen floor, tears and mucus pooling together.

"What is wrong with you?" my mother asked, but I didn't answer. All I knew was that I was never going to take that bus home again— ever. I'd walk the mile and a half in rain and snow before I'd get on it again.

I never got rid of my fear, but in time it abated. I stopped thinking about it. That is, until Shelby and her family were murdered; then it intensified. I was 16. Shelby, who was white, had played tennis with my younger sister, Suzanne. I hadn't known Shelby, not even by name, before she was murdered. Nobody knew what had happened to her and her family for weeks. Rumors circulated. Some people said it was a Mafia hit—that their throats had been cut open and their tongues pulled out through the slits. That it had to do with drugs. Why else would somebody kill an entire family a few days before Christmas? The papers reported it differently: Shelby was found lying naked on her bed, her formal dress over her. The house was smoldering; a fire had been set but hadn't taken off. It had just charred her body, her father's body, her mother's body and her brother's body. Her dog was found dead, too. Smoke inhalation, the police report said.

When the police released the sketch of the man they thought did it, I recognized him, or at least I thought I did. He looked like everybody who lived around me. The black community was in an uproar; the sketch was too generic, they said. A nondescript black man. And it was. Black men were stopped left and right and questioned. I didn't think many whites thought twice about that, though. I knew I didn't. The police knew what they were doing. And to my relief, they finally caught the man. They filled him with bullets. He jerked up from where he had been sitting, spun around, fired a few shots back and then collapsed on the floor.

There was nobody left to convict, nobody left to try, so they went after his mother. Imagine that, his mother as guilty of that crime as he was. Years later the city found out the truth: The man had acted alone. One of the detectives had planted evidence in the case; he had put her fingerprints on a gas can that had been found in the house. The mother was released from jail shortly thereafter.

My fear was most prominent when I was on the subway. There always seemed to be a vagrant with skin that didn't look as if it had aged but had been desiccated from sleeping in one of the cars. I averted my eyes; I thought if I looked at them, they would wake up and ask me what exactly I thought I was looking at. If I felt so much pity, why didn't I do something about it? So I kept my hands in my lap and read the poetry or the plastic-surgery advertisements on the rectangular billboards that paneled the train.

One day on the subway, a black teen-ager sitting next to me put his hand on my knee. I was afraid to tell him to remove it. He started to stroke my leg, rubbing higher and higher, as I bit down on my lip, trying to focus my attention elsewhere, as if by concentrating hard enough, I could make him disappear. When he didn't stop, I tried to discourage him by pressing my knees closer together and using my backpack to stop his hands from moving higher. I tried to move over, but a large man was seated next to me. The leg stroking continued. He ran his hand up and down my leg until the subway doors opened at 96th Street, and I got off and tried to lose him on the crowded platform.

I could see him standing a few yards from me. Did he think I liked his touching me? I didn't know what to do. Another train had come into the station; I decided not to get on it as he'd only follow, so I went over to the pay phone, deposited a quarter and dialed my own num-ber. "Hello?" I said when I was greeted by my answering machine, and I started to talk and laugh, positioning myself so that I could see him. His eyes went from me to his fingernails, from subway cars coming into the station back to me. A few cars later, he took one last look at me and finally boarded. I could still feel him after he left.

It was then that my sister was robbed, her hands bound to the rock-ing chair in her apartment, tape over her mouth. My father asked the question I wanted to but didn't. A question I yelled at him for asking.
"Was he black?"
My sister yelled at him, too, but when he persisted, answered him. "Yes."

I stopped reading the newspaper because I saw the man I dreamt about on every page. I saw a woman's face on the nightly news; it was just a sketch, as the woman had been too badly beaten in Central Park for her face to be shown, too badly beaten to be identified. A woman in a coma. "Do you know her?" the newscaster was asking, and I wanted to call him to say, *Yes, it's me.*
I had been in Central Park the day it happened, within 20 feet of where she was attacked, an hour before she was attacked. When they released the attacker's sketch, I crawled up close to the TV to get a better look at the guy. Had I seen him in the park? Had he been the guy on the bike that had almost hit me as I walked one of the paths? Had I walked over the rock he used to slam her over the head?

I was not afraid of the black men I knew, several of whom lived in our dormitory. At night I often joined the women on my floor at the pub in the basement of our building. I didn't feel particularly close to them. I knew it was not easy for them to have a conversation with me. At that time my thoughts went only in one direction—down—so I rarely spoke when I was with them. My lips held themselves in an unnatural smile, resembling toy wax lips, I imagined.
One night as I sat on a barstool drinking beer, mesmerized by the smoke a young woman across from me was exhaling, a light-skinned black man walked in. I noticed him immediately; he was beautiful, with a strong jaw, something I always notice. He was tall and muscular, too;

his two friends seemed to disappear beside him. I caught his eye, and he smiled and came over.

"Michael," he said, extending his hand. While I shook it, he used his other hand to hoist himself onto a chair.

"Jennifer," I said. I was glad I had finished at least one beer. It soothed me, made me calm. Michael ordered himself a beer and asked if I wanted one.

"I'm okay," I said.

He scanned the room as I picked the label off my bottle of beer, not knowing what to say or do next.

"So, what do you do?" he asked.

"What do I do? Not much."

He looked at me. Then he began talking about himself, about how he had grown up in the Midwest and hadn't been to New York before being accepted to Columbia, where he was working on his M.B.A. Whenever he took a sip of beer, his shirtsleeves rose, and I blushed, looking at his arms. They were thick and hardened.

"You're awfully quiet," he said.

"I know," I said apologetically. "It's just, well, I never know what to say to people when I meet them for the first time."

"Then we'll have to meet again," he said.

That Saturday he took me to dinner and then to a jazz bar. He was better dressed than I was, in a sports coat and khaki pants. I had on a pair of jeans and an old sweater.

I enjoyed having dinner with him. He talked more than I did, about his family mostly. He asked me a few questions that I replied to in short, fragmented sentences, and he nodded encouragingly. I was sure he could see I was nervous, though I doubted he could guess why. It wasn't because he was black; it was because I felt I was hiding things.

I wanted to ask him questions, questions I knew would dehuman-ize, objectify him: *What is it like to be black?* But it wasn't answers I wanted; what I wanted was for him to understand.

By the time we got to the bar, I had had a drink or two and felt energized. Sitting in that chair, I started to feel discriminated against, oppressed; I had become part of a taboo. I wanted people to look at me, to look at us, to see what I had done. I who constantly worried I was racist had finally conquered racism: I no longer saw color. And I was willing to take on the oppression, the discrimination, to be with Michael. It was as if by being with him, I was somehow part of *them*, that I had erased my color, which in turn erased some of my guilt. After all, how could I be racist if I was with him? None of those people in the bar could understand how I felt, I imagined. How I felt about Michael. If people couldn't accept my being with him, well, then I wanted nothing to do with them, either. Oh, if only my parents could see me now!

Standing on the subway platform on our way home, I was no longer afraid. I was no longer afraid because I was with Michael.

Later that night, when he kissed me goodnight, for some reason it surprised me that I did not taste his color on my lips. And it surprised me even more when I did not feel his color as I rested my hand on his arm.

That night as I got ready for bed, I didn't think about the man who came to me through my dreams. It was as if I had finally won him over. What had made that man most angry was that I did not see him, that he had been nothing more than a shadow, something I could step over without noticing I had done it. He was something I could choose to notice or not. How could he say that now? I was doing what he wanted me to do: I was seeing him through Michael.

I dared turn the light off. At first I was uneasy, as if he were there, as if I could sense him. But soon I began to relax, believing he was no longer coming to hurt me. He was just there as he always had been. Just there to see what happened. And he had forgiven me, at least in part.

Michael and I went out a few more times, but it was apparent we had little in common. I was still as drawn to him as ever, but emotionally we never grew closer. There was something resting between us that neither of us wanted to try to conquer first. One of the white women in my dormitory offhandedly mentioned that Michael had asked her out a few months earlier, but she had said no. And then she named a few others he had asked out—all white—before having met me.

The spell was broken. I hadn't gone over to his side; he had come over to mine. I meant nothing to him. I was replaceable, interchangeable. He, too, had been using me for my color! I didn't want to be his way out; I wanted him to be mine.

We went out once more, but by then the spark had gone out. We both felt it. It had just flickered and died.

I didn't call him again, nor did he call me.

For the next few weeks, I spent as much time as possible in the library. I hated sitting around in my dorm room. It made me lonely. I missed the house I grew up in, the familiarity of it.

One night I fell asleep in the library while trying to get through my weekly reading assignments. I had piled books at my feet, picking one up at a time, reading as much as I could until I was so fatigued I thought if only I closed my eyes for a few minutes I'd have the energy to read when I opened them. When I woke, all I could see when I looked out the window and into the darkness was my reflection and that of the lights behind me.

I debated calling security for an escort but then decided against it. I could walk along the sidewalk outside the Manhattan School of Music, which had cameras and guards inside the building monitoring them.

Outside I pulled my jacket tighter as the wind wound itself around Manhattan. Students came in and out of the shops around campus, but as I headed north, I saw fewer and fewer people. Soon there was nobody ahead of me. I took a deep breath.

It was always there that I began to panic, that part of the walk where there was nothing, no cameras, no people, just buildings. Every now and then, a car zipped past, but I doubted any of them would stop if something should happen. They'd just turn their heads and floor the accelerator. Up ahead was where I turned to get under the Manhattan School of Music cameras. Only a few blocks left.

I let out my breath when I got there safely. There was one more isolated stretch—no more than a block, really—but my building was right next to a park that had crack vials all over the place. Sometimes I wished I could sit up in a tree and watch what went on there at night. I was as fascinated as I was scared. Whenever I walked by the park at night, I imagined somebody coming out from there with a needle in hand. I walked faster.

I decided to walk in the street to be in the headlights of oncoming traffic. I tightened the straps of my backpack. As I got closer to my dormitory, I saw three black men coming down the street, talking loudly and animatedly. My body tensed up, as if bear-hugging itself. I tried to make myself look bigger. I tried to make myself look deter-mined. Instinctively I crossed the street to let them pass. It wasn't until I heard my name being called that I realized one of them was Michael. I knew that nondescript black man would be back.

Jennifer Jeanne Patterson *received her M.F.A. from Columbia University. She currently lives in Minneapolis, where she is working on her novel "Twenty Trees."*

Silver Redhorse

Hal Herring

Moulder Branch connected to Hurricane Creek, which fed into the Flint River much farther away than a person could hope to reach without a driver's license. The Flint, in turn, made its loops away from the mountains through flat cotton and soybean country to pour into the Tennessee. This connection was immensely important, because it meant that big-water fish—river drum, carp, even striped bass and sauger, which we called jack salmon—could find their way during high water upstream into the hinterlands, where the water was born of limestone caverns and dark seeps in the low, flat-topped foothills of Alabama's Cumberlands. I liked old ponds, their quiet waters weedy and concealing, trembling with the movements of bass and shellcrackers. But no mystery on earth meant as much to me when I was 14 as that system of creeks and small rivers braiding toward the Tennessee.

Moulder Branch began as Sneed Spring, a crystal-clear stream that emerged from a shadowed, fern-hung hole in a small cliff, one visible vein of a thousand that coursed unseen through the heart of the mountains. The rocks on its bed were covered with a black-green moss that shivered in the current, and small clouds of bright-colored dace and sculpin swept up into the darkness of the cave and back out into the sunlight, joined at times by other minnows who followed an opposite life and had no color at all, were clear as glass. If you could catch them, you could watch their organs working through their skin—yellow stomach, blue heart, blue brain.

During the third week of March, schools of spawning silver red-horse appeared on the gravel beds and shoals of Moulder Branch, about four miles below the cave. The creek at this point had been joined by the waters of two more large wet-weather springs and several washes and was about 20 feet wide, although it shrank to a trickle in the late summer. The redhorse were members of the lowly sucker family that spent most of their lives in the deep holes of the Flint River or in the giant Tennessee. Their traveling habits lent them a profound air of mystery, the attraction of the wanderer from far away who appears suddenly and gives beauty and energy to a creek that was, in its middle reaches, pretty ordinary. They were a striking red color in the clear water and ranged in size from a foot or so to about 20 inches. They traveled in schools of dozens, and in such a small and seasonal creek, they presented an amazing sight. To a boy who longed for trout and salmon, for wild Alaskan rivers, they were a priceless gift. I began to watch for them the first week of March, just after the close of rabbit season, when the trees were just beginning to bud. The pounding of rain on the roof above my bed would awaken me late at night, and I would imagine them, lifting up from the dark gravel beds and mussel piles deep in the muddy Tennessee, catching the taste of the rising waters there in Moulder Branch, a taste of rich loam washed down through sinkholes in the mountains, bloodroot, ginseng, polished limestone, the scent of subterranean creatures.

As I watched for them, I dreamed of the wonders that they must be passing in their journey: sunken barges, alligator turtles, catfish as big as a man, lost relics of war and human endeavor. From the muddy channel of the Tennessee they moved up into the Flint, where the water was stained red from the clay of the cotton fields, and the thick primeval salamanders called hellbenders drifted above a rocky bed strewn with potsherds and stone arrowheads. The Flint suffered from the runoff of a mixture of chemicals that we called simply "cotton poison," and I don't think the redhorse lingered there. It was another 20 river miles to the mouth of Hurricane Creek and at least 15 more to the mouth of Moulder. I don't know when they started this journey each year, or how long it took them, but what they accomplished each spring was nothing less than a passage between worlds.

At that time in my life, I was intensely solitary, by choice and design. I have since struggled in fiction to capture the feeling that pervades my memories of those creeks and that landscape and that age. I felt then that I also passed between worlds that had distinct boundaries.

I had good friends at school, but I hated the confinement of school to the point that I was often physically ill. I never considered playing any sports that would require me to spend even one extra minute on the grounds of the school, and I rushed home to go immediately out walking or hunting or fishing. My real life, the one in which I felt at ease, was on the creeks and in the woods and along the edges of the fields, and I didn't feel any need to share it. After the exhausting raucousness of a day of junior high, the silence of that world was like falling into a feather bed. Because even then landowners were jealous of their hunting rights and property lines, I was often trespassing, and my wanderings were best kept to the thickets and the woods. I traveled a lot during hunting season in the low beds of washes, following the tracks of coon and fox and coyote. Like them, I didn't much care for open ground.

The place where Moulder Branch pours into Hurricane is narrow enough to leap across, and when I knew it best, it was partially blocked by a gradually tilting sycamore 3 feet through. The water had gouged a deep hole beneath the roots of the tree, and during floods it poured over the pistol-butted trunk, and the whole tree vibrated out to the tips of its branches. When the water dropped and changed from brown to translucent green, I could straddle the sycamore and watch for the flash of redhorse feeding in the hole. Until they reached the shallow spawning grounds, they would take a night crawler or red worm fished directly on the bottom, and I usually caught quite a few from the side of the creek opposite the sycamore, where the bank was low enough to land them. These fish I always released, because the hook in the mouth did not mortally injure them, and I didn't really like to eat them. They were bony in the extreme, although between the bones, the flesh was white and firm. I eventually learned to pressure-cook them, a process that melts the smaller bones, but by then it seemed like too much trouble.

Later in the month, when the redhorse moved farther up the creek, the only way to take them was by "snatching"—that is, snagging them with a treble hook. I also hunted them with a light bow and old aluminum arrows, with frog gigs, homemade spears and a pistol loaded with .22 shorts. With these methods, catch-and-release was not an option.

The spawning grounds were along a section of creek lined with big red oaks and hackberries, with a thicket of sumac and locust saplings taking over a cow pasture on one bank and a cornfield on the other. It was one of the best places in the valley to hunt fox squirrels, which didn't leave their nests until midmorning and foraged in the corn rather than frantically gathering nuts in the woods like their gray cousins. The redhorse gathered on a long, dangerously shallow gravel bed, with shoal water below, where the riffles would hide them if need be until they could reach a deeper section below a cut bank. No ospreys or eagles lived in that part of Alabama, and the trees on both banks met high above the water, shielding them from hawks. In days past, a lot of people, tenant farmers and sharecroppers who did not ignore free fish, came to take them with seines and treble hooks, but the land around there had actually lost population since the '50s, and those who remained were bent on other tasks. Although I never saw anyone other than myself fishing there, all the local old-timers who saw me knew exactly what I was doing.

The trick was to thread the brush and flood trash to the edge of the creek without spooking the whole school, cast the single treble across almost to the other side and let it roll slightly downstream. Then you twitched it, reeling in about 6 inches of line, almost exactly like working a plastic worm for bass. The redhorse varied widely in size, and you tried to pick an individual fish to snag. The hookup was usually not a great surprise, but because they were often hooked in the tail, and the right fish could weigh up to 4 pounds, the fight was dramatic and worthwhile. The struggle would put the whole school immediately to flight. Usually I would make several probing casts into the hole under the cut bank and take a couple more that way. After that, it would be time to walk, seek another gravel bed where another group was holding, or try whatever holes could be found along the way. A lot of times I would leave my rod and reel stashed along the creek somewhere and go off looking for snakes or studying the plants that came up specifically at that time. The fields and hedgerows that would be a jungle by mid-May were still bare or just beginning to green, but the delicate plants of the woods' floor were already at the height of their flowering. The muted power of the March sun, falling unhindered through the leafless trees, was perfect for hepatica, trillium, troutlily, bloodroot. Later, when the trees had leafed and the tough plants of the fields were in full riot, these plants would have passed their prime and be barely noticeable beneath the deep shade of the oaks.

One afternoon, waiting for the redhorse to come back up onto the gravel, I heard a tremendous splash, and an eight-point whitetail buck came galloping down the creek, ran off the shoal into the deep, and swam below me, not a yard from my feet. Nothing was chasing him that I could see, and when he left the creek, he walked away slowly into the thicket.

Bow fishing for redhorse was not too different from snatching with a treble hook if you shot from the bank. Except for the fact that at 14 it was still wonderful to be out in the world with a powerful weapon rather than a fishing rod. The height of sport with the bow was to wade up behind the fish, which was almost impossible and which I accomplished only twice that I remember. Shooting into deep water was difficult because of the refraction problem, and when you did manage to hit one, you usually were in for a soaking when you went in after it. I had a bow-fishing rig, a coffee can wound with braided line and held to the bow with a long bolt and a piece of flatiron. You could buy a special fishing arrow with a hole in front of the nock where you tied on the line. The first time I ever used this rig, I shot at a very large and very expensive grass carp that a neighbor had bought to control algae in his catfish pond. I saw the enormous fish, went home, got the rig and came back, obsessed. The first shot launched the heavy arrow about 10 feet before the braided line wrapped around my forearm, peeled off the skin all the way to my wrist, and then brought the arrow winging back at my face. The grass carp lived through this attempt.

So I hunted redhorse with regular aluminum arrows, the older the better, because they could survive only so many strikes into the rocks of the bottom. Broadheads hit the water and veered off to either side, so I used target points or the special flats I made up for hunting rabbits, with a .38 brass fitted over the tip. A strike anywhere in front of the dorsal fin killed the fish outright, and they could be retrieved easily as they drifted along, slowed by the dragging of the arrow.

Why, when I so loved to see the living redhorse on the shoal, did I need to kill them? Why would I wait for them, dream of their passage, depend on them as the true harbingers of beloved spring, and still creep up to the cut bank, point my cheap pistol down at the shallow water and shoot the biggest one I saw?

The question certainly never occurred to me then. (It might help to know that during those years I often lost the first fish of every trip simply because I was so anxious to begin fishing that I could not finish my knots correctly.) Only in recent years, after an intense and continuing apprenticeship in the art of finding game and taking fish, have I begun to wonder how it is that bloodlust and the love of nature could be so inextricably wound for me. During most of that apprenticeship, the desire to touch whatever was my quarry was foremost and assumed. Stints on commercial fishing boats (jobs I gleefully took on because they offered the chance to fish for fun during breaks and while traveling to and from the fishing grounds), working in seafood packing houses, and a very brief time hunting coyotes for hides, caused me to realize early that my very soul was imperiled by viewing living creatures as potential cash money. This view requires that the seeker abandon any concepts of the sacred nature of the creature sought and ignore its attendant mysteries in an attempt to bring it to hand in a practical and efficient manner. A swordfish, which is one of the greatest predators ever to swim the waters of creation, brings $4.75 a pound. A coyote, which you have followed and watched as it hunts mice, does inexplicable dances in morning sunlight and calls out in bizarre cadences to its fellows, brings $55 to $60, which beats wages working for someone else and allows you to wander around on the grasslands all during the late winter without looking like the slacker you probably are. Your .22 bullet takes the coyote in the brain while he is thinking... what? You have no time to ponder; you must immediately go looking for the next one. Rent is due; the clutch is going out in the truck. Reverence falls by the wayside. You cannot serve two gods at once. Sadly enough for me, since I live in good country and am usually unemployed, I believe that paid guiding for fish and game falls under the same cloud.

But what about killing for free? What about snatching spawning redhorse with a treble hook? I can only say that I had not evolved past the point where I wished mightily to hold in my hands the mystery that fascinated me. I still haven't. I most appreciate the journey of the redhorse, the clear cave waters of the spawning grounds, the distant, muddy, secret world of its home, when I snag it, fight it, and hold it in my hands. Maybe it is the substance of creation that I want to touch. Trying to find a way to catch them, I studied them more closely than I ever would, had my interest been only in seeing them. This has proven true with every fish and animal I have ever sought to kill. The mystery expands as one enters it, like opening a door into a castle or entering a cave. Snatching redhorse, I was out on the creek almost every day for the three weeks the fish were there. I knew every hole, gravel bar, cut bank. I saw the same copperhead three times, the same crows, deer, skunks, the same trees until I knew each one individually, and I can see them all in my mind right now. It is in this study, this knowing, that reverence for the whole of the world that sustains us is born. This reverence can make us stronger, less careless, less destructive. It is a clear, good thing. I am grateful that I do not have to try to live without it.

Anyone may by now be justified in asking what I did with the redhorse that I snagged, shot, speared and so on. I strung them through the gills on a forked green ash or willow stick and dragged them up to the paved road that ran along the foot of the mountains at the far side of the cove where we lived. A mile or so back, there was a deep hollow, with another small spring creek, where an old man named Fred Johnson and his wife, Sary, held out in a partially collapsed log cabin. No one used the scrubby pasture of the hollow, and the cabin had been abandoned for 20 years. They owned no land, did no work that I knew of, paid no rent. A much larger clapboard house had stood at one time at the mouth of the hollow, closer to the road, and the old couple had lived in it for a while with an assortment of other relatives, but someone had burned it to the ground, and everyone had scattered except for them.

Fred and Sary Johnson lived without electricity or plumbing in the one, tight room of the cabin, growing turnips in the yard, foraging, killing coons and possums. They kept an assortment of "catch dogs," small, often mangy feists that attacked whatever wildlife presented itself and relieved Mr. Johnson of the need to kill game with .22 cartridges, which cost money. These dogs were locally famous for disappearing and giving Mr. Johnson an excuse to travel far and wide in search of them across private lands otherwise off limits to his hunting. That was how I met him, far off in a place called Duskins Hollow, where we both were trespassing, looking for ginseng. When I arrived with the red-horse, Sary was usually sitting quietly on the porch in an old reclining lawn chair, wrapped in blankets against the chill of the March afternoon, the front door open, and a hot fire barely lighting the dark room behind her. She greeted me but did not usually rise from her cocoon. Mr. Johnson was usually there with her or within shouting distance in the woods. He was jovial, with a little bit of the friendliness of the con man in him. Sometimes he was reeling and red-faced with drink. He was seriously happy to get the fish. Once, he went back with me to the shoals where I had caught them and snatched some from under the cut bank with a willow pole, 10 feet of string and a treble hook that he borrowed from me and later returned.

Mr. Johnson had rebuilt an old flume that carried water from a seep spring by the cabin into a concrete cattle trough, and he cleaned the redhorse on a plank set over the outflow from the trough. If he was sober, he took a shovel and buried the offal carefully at the edge of the woods; otherwise, he flung it far and wide as he talked. I never hung around long, and I don't remember how they cooked the fish, though I guess it must have been on a rack over the fireplace. Once the next fall when I met him on the road, he gave me two enormous ginseng roots, bigger than any I had ever seen, and I wore one of them on a string around my neck for a while, until too many people at school asked what it was. A year later, the Johnsons were gone, and a year after that, some deer hunters took over the cabin, used it for a few weekends, and burned it down.

It would be easy to close this story, or essay, or whatever it is, with a litany of destruction: cabins burned, creeks channelized, housing developments planned, the redhorse gone as surely as are Fred and Sary Johnson. And I could, in truth, write it that way. The fields on either side of Moulder Branch were sold to a farmer who was a devotee of clean farming, and he did channelize all the washes and scraped them clear of the hedgerows that had been the nesting place of quail and bluebirds and just about everything else. I met him once, and he looked out over the scarified land and said to me, "I've put a lot into this place, but I've just about got it looking like I want it to." His efforts inspired the county to go on a campaign of its own, spraying herbicide on the hedgerows along the roads, laying in culverts, straightening side creeks. The runoff moved too fast down into

Moulder Branch, and the bed of the creek no longer held enough water in the spring for the redhorse to spawn. Although Sneed Spring produces as much water as ever, during the summer the middle reaches of the creek are entirely dry. The lands all along the creek are leased for big money to urban deer hunters who brook no trespass on their investment. It is a stricter, balder, less sheltering world.

But, true to its ability to inspire my lifelong reverence, it is by no means a delicate world. The redhorse are there still, though they are limited now to the main branch of Hurricane Creek. March a year ago I was 32 years old, and home for a visit. My nephew, 8, was there with my sister. It was a close, warm day, building overcast, and I could feel the fall of the barometer in my sinuses. We rummaged through the equipment shed and turned up an old spiderweb-encrusted Fenwick spinning rod and a green-and-white ceramic Zebco Cardinal, the finest spinning reel available in 1976. We stripped a Jitterbug of its two big trebles, swapped the line on the Cardinal for fresh 10-pound test, and set off for the creek.

Moulder Branch was too low, even in the hole beneath the bridge, to hold fish of any size. We set off downstream to a place where another big spring comes in and builds the volume of the creek. Nothing there. I was worried that my nephew would tire before we found anything worth catching, but he was excited and up for the walk. I had forgotten how fraught with fantastic possibility a fishing trip can be when you are 8. A long walk down Moulder Branch searching for redhorse can be on a par with any trip to Alaska or the Congo. I wanted to feel the same way, and I did. At the mouth of the creek, where it pours into the main Hurricane, a wide fan of gravel had built up and created a shallows and shoal system that pushed the main channel of Hurricane far over. That main channel was deep, and dark green. The big sycamore at the mouth of Moulder Branch was long washed away, and the hole beneath it was filled with clean gravel. A group of big redhorse came up over the lip of the gravel from the main channel and milled just below us. Smaller fish followed, swept in an entire school over the gravel and back into the channel. "There they are!" I said, thrilled. My nephew was solemn, staring at the fish. He grabbed for the fishing rod in a near frenzy and bungled the first cast, almost landing our only two treble hooks against a logjam. He reeled fast and tried again, this time arcing the hooks over the gravel bed, over the redhorse. "Now," I said, "jerk and reel, not too hard, not too fast. Look, you can see the hooks there, just on the other side of that fish!" He jerked once, exactly right, and the rod bowed. The sound of the creek was the sound of beauty itself. The new leaves on the big hardwoods all around us glowed a dusty green. The light coming down into the water was a pure butter yellow. Off to the south was the thunder of a storm.

Hal Herring *is a native of Alabama and has lived in Montana for the past 12 years. His writing has appeared in* Field & Stream, Atlantic Monthly *and* Bugle, *the magazine of the Rocky Mountain Elk Foundation.*

Familiar Things

Samuel Pickering

For six months the chancellor of the university lived next door. In May he and his family went to DisneyWorld. Each morning Vicki fed his dogs, two Labradors named Mousse and Huckleberry. One morning, after feeding the dogs, Vicki pointed to our kitchen ceiling and said, "Don't you think that's better?"

Last fall in Norwich, Vicki had bought a light fixture for the kitchen. Once home, she discovered the lip of the fixture was warped. For months the lip swayed, dizzying across Vicki's vision. Then in May, while preparing food for Mousse and Huckleberry, Vicki noticed three of the same fixtures in the chancellor's house, none warped. "The darn things only cost $21.95 apiece," she said. "The university should have bought something better." In June the chancellor accepted the presidency of Louisiana State University. "Before he and Clara leave for Louisiana," Vicki said, "I'm going to switch fixtures."

"Don't," I said.

"I'm doing it," she said. "He's leaving, and the change won't bother him. I'd switch fixtures even if he stayed."

A week later when the chancellor was in Baton Rouge, Vicki rid herself of the warped fixture. "I switched ours with the one in the study. I thought about removing the fixture from the master bedroom, but then Clara might have noticed. Women's minds wander to cooking, cleaning, lights, almost anything during—"

"Enough," I said, clapping my hands over my ears and staring down at the kitchen table. "I don't want to hear any more."

Despite refusing to glance at the ceiling, I knew not only what hung above but also what lay ahead. School had ended. Francis was riding a mountain bike in Italy, and Edward and Eliza were at camp in Maine. Summer had arrived, and the time had almost come to depart for Nova Scotia. Every June, Vicki and I debate going to her family's home in Beaver River, Nova Scotia. Invariably we decide to spend summer at home, in Storrs, Conn. Just after the decision, however, something happens, and we leave. Two years in a row, thieves stole my bicycle, and rather than remain in town fuming, we decamped. For a moment I thought the ceiling fixture might push us toward the northern lights. But then the chancellor didn't notice the switch. Four days later he and Clara invited us to a farewell party. At the party the kitchen light flickered in my mind. In hopes of dimming fluorescent consciousness, I squeezed a skin of red wine dry. For a while I succeeded in darkening awareness, becoming an incandescent bore. An acquaintance's nose was so large, I informed a vice president of the university, that he couldn't blow it without packing his nostrils with gunpowder. After the naiads finished bathing, I asked a dean, what service did the dryads provide? On the man's looking puzzled, I explained that the dryads distributed towels.

A sociologist, not a classicist, the man didn't appreciate my bon mot. Consequently, I asked him a riddle. Why is the letter *B* like a hot fire? As the answer—because it makes *oil boil*—did not elevate him to laughter, I then described recent doings in Carthage. One chilly night in February, Horace Armitage staggered into Enos Mayfield's Inn and sat by the stove. Horace had prepared for the cold by swallowing a pint of homemade antifreeze before leaving his house. Nevertheless, the walk chilled him, and he hunkered over the stove, rubbing his hands together and spreading his fingers. "Mr. Armitage," Mayfield's son Tyrell said after five minutes. "There ain't no fire in that stove."

"Damn you, you rascal," Horace exclaimed, standing up, shivering. "Why did you tell me that? I was just beginning to get warm. Now you've given me the shakes."

Like pigweed amid corn, my wit proved too weedy for the chancellor's cultivated guests. The dean having left me alone, I ambled over to a clump of people, including, among others, the town's representative in the state legislature. Age had uprooted several incumbents, and local Democrats, she said, were having trouble finding people to plant on the town council. At this furrow of the conversation, wine blighted my intelligence. Eight minutes later, the representative led me into town hall to be interviewed by the Democratic Committee. The committee sat soberly around a table. I thumped down, slapping a plastic glass brimming with wine in front of me. I began discussion by apologizing for being "tight as a tick." I announced that I wouldn't hesitate to raise taxes, saying I'd promise the citizenry a chicken in every garage and a Lexus in every pot, wit that brought puzzled, not smiling, looks. Afterward, remarks vanished in a Cabernet Sauvignon haze. Eventually my stomach turned feathery, and I walked home through the woods, suffering from dyspepsia, "the remorse," my friend Josh said later, "of a guilty palate."

The next morning I informed Vicki the time had come to leave for Nova Scotia. By summer's end my lubricated appearance at town hall would have dried and blown from mind. "Maybe," Vicki said, "but suppose the Democrats nominate you? Drunk or sober, you'd lead the ticket."

"Surely," I said, "the committee wouldn't nominate a tippler."

"Bad behavior provides the best possible education for office," Vicki continued. "The pure and the good cannot cope with public matters. Besides, you behaved like a jackass, something that always indicates good character. No man who has been laughed at is irredeemably damned."

Four days later, Vicki and I, and George and Penny, the dogs, left Connecticut, driving to Bar Harbor and the new ferry to Yarmouth. By the time I reached New Hampshire, I'd shed the cloven hoof kicked up at town hall. In truth, banging the boards of my stall frees me to spend summers willfully. Misbehavior protects a person from distending ambition. Instead of foundering amid the poor provender of position and responsibility, I wander pastures that have nourished me since childhood. Any wise man, as Josh put it, can run a college, but only a fool can lead the good life. "Shakespeare was wrong," I said to Vicki as we passed Portsmouth. "Pharmacists are not *pillers* of society. Essayists are."

"What?" Vicki said.

"Never mind," I said, dropping the speed to 50 mph.

Vicki and I are experienced dog travelers. At Mackey's in Willimantic, Vicki bought a pillow cover, stuffing it afterward with two pillows purchased at Penny's, making a dog bed for $28, $31 less than a comparable bed at Puppy Love, the pet store in East Brook Mall. We walked and watered the dogs throughout the drive: at the "Welcome to Maine" rest stop near York; outside the Birchwood Motel north of Castine; across a field behind the Dexter Shoe Outlet in Ellsworth, Maine, where boat shoes sold for $39, unfortunately none 10½, Vicki's size; then finally along the hill above the Bay Ferries terminal at Bar Harbor. Dog days are tiring. The owner of Birchwood kept two cats. During nights the cats pounce from the railing running the length of the motel, landing on the hoods of cars. To prevent the cats leaping onto the Toyota and conducting the dogs in a chorus of howls, I parked 10 feet from the railing. Still, at 5:12 the next morning, a cat ambled across the parking lot and Penny yelped. At least she yelped until I joined her in the car, barefoot and wearing pajamas.

Later that morning Vicki and I planned to explore Castine. Because the day was hot, we didn't leave the dogs in the car long, this despite cracking all four windows and placing a plastic bowl of water on the floor in front of the driver's seat. Still, we wandered a bit. ABCD Books sold used books. A customer in the store asked the clerk the location of books describing nature. The clerk didn't know. "Next to gardening," I said, having roamed the store searching for one of my books.

"Any collection of my essays would have done," I told Vicki later.

"You write about New England. Did you really expect to find one of your books?" she said, handing me a postcard, adding, "Here's a present. I bought it at a souvenir stand." Six belted Galloways grazed across the front of the card, the white bands resembling corsets circling the stomachs of the steers. I pondered buying a muffin and a cup of coffee at Cappy's Bakery. I wanted to stroll down Commercial to the Megunticook River. I planned to sit on a bench and sip and munch. I imagined furling into the quiet and watching schooners slide through the harbor. "Sweets and doldrums kill dogs," Vicki said, steering me clear of reverie and piloting me back to the car. The ferry at Bar Harbor was a catamaran, from the side looking like a pasteboard iron, from the front, a giant ray, wings sweeping black toward the water. On board I sat in the theater. Tired from having muzzled Penny before breakfast, I slept through a showing of "Anastasia," waking only for the death of Rasputin.

"If your heart is in the Highlands," Josh informed a musical acquaintance, "it ain't here." In Nova Scotia, my heart and body can almost always be found in Beaver River. Once or twice during the summer, envy causes a chamber to skip, when, for example, a friend writes from

Italy or France, his letter winy with murmuring about Tuscany or the Loire Valley. A walk, however, soon restores rhythm, ambles along the drumlin overlooking the Bay of Fundy being natural pacemakers.

Electrical problems always await us in Beaver River. The hot-water heater in the house is 44 years old. This summer it needed, as the repairman phrased it, an "electrical bypass." After the operation, I bathed, sinking under a white mound of "Wild Rose" bubbles. Before the bath, while the heater was convalescent, I'd spent days doing chores in and out of the house—inside, removing shutters, freeing stuck sashes, and jacking up the backhouse in order to open the pantry door. Vicki admires spiders, and before I vacuumed, she urged me to be gentle. "Catch the spiders and take them outside," she instructed. "They are fragile. Be careful not to suck them up when they scurry into cracks. Cleaning near spiders requires a delicate touch." Many spiders built webs under windows, bays being favorites. The spiders fed on flies and wood lice, spotting boards under webs yellow with droppings, the exoskeletons of lice drifting dry and broken across the floor like minute shields. The vacuum cleaner wheezed when I turned it on. During the winter a mouse built a nest in the tank, crawling up a 7-foot hose at the end of which was a metal extension shaped like a boomerang.

The second morning in Beaver River I cut rhubarb growing along the stone wall beside Ma's Property, the field south of the house. Later Vicki bought a flat of strawberries grown in Annapolis Valley. The next day she made eight jars of strawberry-rhubarb preserves. I spent much of the first week in Nova Scotia outside. From under the bays I trimmed bridal wreath. I oiled the scythe and mowed grass behind the barn. I cut dead branches from hawthorns and dragged away spruce weakened by porcupines, then snapped by wind. I chopped Japanese knotweed with a machete, carting canes into the woods. Forty years prior, Vicki's father had planted the knotweed as an ornamental, a mistake because the plant spreads by rhizomes, forming dark, close bacterial thickets that smother other vegetation. Two red maples shade the front of the house. In fall they drop leaves into trenches formed where gables pitch up from the roof. Moss and twigs cling together in heaps, and the trenches become planters. This past year asters rooted, and soon after arriving in Nova Scotia I climbed atop the bays and weeded the roof, hoeing some of the soil, then using a long, bamboo pole to pry up the rest, playing clumps of dirt like fish on lines.

In summer, saws jump to hand. After a morning's cutting, be the slicing useful or whimsical and indulgent, I drink coffee and eat a sugar doughnut. Rocking in the kitchen, a wood fire thumping in the stove, I feel more attuned to the world than in Connecticut. Instead of hanging heavy, leaded with the metallic fumes of automobiles, air sweeps blue off the Bay of Fundy and, stirring through the side meadow, whisks up currents of rose and pine. In Nova Scotia, summers slip together seamlessly, the appointments of days comfortable and familiar.

On our arrival, black alder and sheep laurel bloomed along the lane leading to the bluff. As I do each summer, I confused black alder with inkberry. Once more, sheep laurel startled me, the small blossoms, cups overflowing with pink sweetened by purple. A long-horned beetle alit on my right leg as I sat on the side porch. A white-spotted sawyer, the beetle feeds on dead and dying conifers. During the summer several sawyers land on me. "Because," Vicki explained, "you are so woodenly conventional." The first moth I noticed this summer was an underwing with three glossy black spots dotting the margin of its forewing. The moth is common. In past years I tried unsuccessfully to identify it. This summer I failed again. For creatures about the farm, place is constant, something that reassures the two-leggers who live in the house.

Every summer a song sparrow or one of her progeny nests in the rugosa roses bordering the side meadow. Caterpillars of mourning cloak butterflies chew the willow at the edge of the meadow ratty. Batches of their castoff skins stick to the ends of branches, turning twigs black and spiky. This summer in the blueberry field, a stick mimic clung to a stem of fireweed. A fleshy shelf jutted from behind a caterpillar's head like a leaf scar. While the caterpillar's back legs grasped a twig, a silk thread tied the insect's head to a leaf. The head stuck out, resembling a bud, and the caterpillar's legs twisted like crooked twigs from its body. I wouldn't have seen the caterpillar if I hadn't known where to look. Every July a similar caterpillar appears in the same patch of fireweed.

Trifles compose place and character. In early afternoon a cock pheasant wandered the lane, usually resting near alders shadowed by apple trees. At dusk a porcupine swam up from beneath the backhouse, or did until I crammed buoys into holes dug under the building. Place and person are patchworks of the small. The more patches a person recognizes, the more he will appreciate life. Great achievement deceives, often leading to dissatisfaction. During my first amble along the lane, I heard the song of a white-throated sparrow, then those of myrtle and black-throated green warblers. Tails bobbing, a small flock of palm warblers foraged low through scrub. A black-backed gull rode the wind over the headland, muttering impatiently, the sounds out of feather with the bird's unperturbed, elegant flight. Two eiders and a loon bobbled in the water, the breast of this last ballooning white, like a buoy. Two years ago I lay two sheets of plywood on the open ground behind the headland. While four brown snakes curled like laces under one sheet, a vole nested under the other.

A white admiral patrolled the lane. Soon Atlantic fritillaries would sip meadowsweet in George's Field, and monarchs would perch lazily on knapweed growing above the foundation hole on Ma's Property. Deerflies had hatched, and looking at the ground, I watched their shadows swing around my head. Suddenly the sour aroma of witherod oozed through the air. Bill Grace, our neighbor, had sawed branches off saplings that leaned into the lane. As the leaves of witherod blackened, fragrance clotted and fermented, repulsing Vicki but appealing to me, smacking of bourbony bread pudding. For 12 years Bill's cat has crossed the highway and hunted our property. Amid grass along the lane lay pieces of two meadow jumping mice, the tufts of their tails small black brooms. A northern harrier lifted herself over white spruce, then slid down the headland. Near a setting of swamp candles lay the head of a hare, hunks of meat red and still attached, fur spreading in a brown puddle, scraps left by a great horned owl. I pocketed the head and later stuck it in a jar, covering it with a blend of water and Javex 2, an all-fabric bleach.

Even the new seemed familiar. Cardinals nested at the edge of the blueberry field, the first Vicki and I ever saw in Beaver River. In the lane a large green-and-yellow dragonfly hawked a skimmer out of the air. Perched on a twig, the big dragonfly ate its smaller cousin. The dragonfly swallowed the skimmer head first, eating everything except the wings, which hung near its jaws for a moment before falling and drifting away. Torpid after the meal, the dragonfly didn't flutter when I pushed it off its perch onto my index finger. Later I surprised a woodcock and two fledglings in the damp near the cow pond. That afternoon the body of a humpbacked whale washed ashore at Beaver River. Rot had shrunk the whale's head, and the carcass was smallish, 12 paces from front to fluke. Time had flayed the body, slicing black skin into strips that waved in the tide like kelp. Beneath the skin gleamed hunks of yellow-and-brown flesh. Blubber glistened, and cables of bone bound the animal's sides. From the sides, fins swept out like loose, knobby wings. When I turned away, Penny bathed in the carcass. "No different from last summer when she rolled in dead seal," Vicki said later. The next day Vicki's brother Geoff arrived for a visit, and we pried two vertebrae from the body. After inserting a long pole through holes left by the spinal column, we brought the vertebrae back to the house, each of us carrying an end of the pole. "By next summer the stench should be gone," Vicki said.

Keeping life familiar takes effort. Grass grows amid the stones above the outlet at Beaver River. Vicki's father thought the grass was foxtail, and for years Vicki and her father cut clumps, arranging them in vases in his study. After her father's death, Vicki continued to cut the grass. Every July foxtails evoke memories of family summers past. For years I've known that the grass Vicki and her father cut was squirrel tail, not foxtail, a lovely but, as botanists put it, "noxious weed." Never have I corrected Vicki when she called the grass foxtail. Better that familiar association endures, tying daughter to father, warming days with recollection.

Things that occur in Nova Scotia seem to have happened before. One morning Vicki picked 1,304 blueberries. That night she started reading "Moby Dick." She began at page 147, the chapter titled "The Mast-Head," having read the first 146 pages two years before. Printed in Boston for the St. Botolph Society, the edition had been given to Vicki's father in 1922 by Aunt Leila. The following night at dusk I walked to the headland. Venus gleamed near the lower horn of the crescent moon. From horn and star, yellow ladders rolled across the water in rungs. Lights from fishing boats pricked the horizon. To the north, waves slipped landward smooth and silver until they broke into shadows and oozed oily over the sand.

Two days later I hiked the cliffs above Bear Cove. Several years before, portions of the movie "The Scarlet Letter" had been filmed at Bear Cove. Atop an outcrop, builders constructed a house and barn.

During the past year, teen-agers tattooed walls with sketches of bats, flying snakes and headless horses. Scattered throughout the house, perhaps as a form of evangelical exorcism, were copies of a religious tract, "How to Live Forever." The front cover of the tract was blue. Pasted against the blue was the skyline of Atlanta, a cross towering above buildings. The tract was distributed by Rock Spring Baptist Church, located at 5900 Reynolds Road in Morrow, Ga., Tommy Aman, Pastor. Printed inside the back cover was an "Eternal Life Birth Certificate." "I," the certificate began, followed by a space for a name, "received Christ at." After a space for the place appeared the word "on," this followed by a final space for the date. Also printed on the certificate was an excerpt from John. "And this is the record, that God hath given to us eternal life, and this is in his Son. These things have I written unto you that believe on in the name of the Son of God; that ye may know that ye have eternal life."

The slow roll of days in Beaver River quickens memory. Early in July while walking the spruce woods behind the headland, I stepped on a young hare. The hare screamed and flipped over, legs kicking spasmodically. I picked the animal up, and wrapping her in folds of my sweatshirt, carried her back to the house. I intended to drive to Yarmouth to buy an eyedropper and soybean milk, the kind of milk fed to unweaned kittens. "I can save this hare," I said.

"No, you can't," Vicki said. "Break her neck and end her suffering."

"Don't thwart good intentions," I said, suddenly remembering when a cat belonging to Vicki's mother ripped a mouse open. The mouse's entrails protruded. I pushed the entrails back through the tear, then asked Vicki to sew the wound, saying I would hold the mouse while she sewed, after which I'd cover the stitches with antibiotic cream. Vicki refused to stitch the wound, and as a result I snapped the mouse's neck, a memory that bothers me every summer. The hare fared better than the mouse. More shocked than hurt, the animal recovered in the warmth of my shirt. After examining the hare's legs, making sure no bones were broken, I returned her to the woods. I rubbed her back, then placed her on the ground. Quickly she jumped away, vanishing under blackberry canes.

The next morning Vicki and I received a letter from Eliza. "Thursday was an exciting day," she began.

For breakfast I decided to be adventurous and have oatmeal instead of raisin bran. I will not be repeating the experiment. The first few bites were good, but the rest tasted like paste. After breakfast I packed for the Lake Magaunacuk canoe trip. I was in the stern of our boat with Sarah in the bow. The rest of my tent went as well as a couple of other girls. When we reached the lake, I saw an extremely large green frog sitting in reeds. The day was sunny, and although I wore sunscreen, I still got burned on my arms. The lake looked deceptively short, but it twisted and lengthened. We paddled for about five hours and covered 3 or 4 miles. Because I provided most of the real pushing power for my canoe, my arms felt like jelly at the end. I was so happy when lunch came. We had cheese Triscuits and Fig Newtons, then went swimming. It was really windy on the way back and hard to paddle, but Sarah, Abby and I belted out show tunes. Consequently we kept drifting off course and were the last to finish.

"That sounds familiar," Vicki said. "Eliza must have lifted the letter from one of your books."

"Yes," I said, "green frogs, Fig Newtons, sentimental old songs, and drifting—that's the good life."

Samuel Pickering *teaches English at the University of Connecticut. Eleven collections of his familiar essays have been published, the most recent being "A Little Fling" and "Deprived of Unhappiness."*

Two Years

Russell Tomlin

*T*ogo, West Africa, is a 335-mile-long, 70-mile-wide chip of country wedged between Ghana and Benin. Hugging the prime meridian at 8 degrees above the equator, Togo operates under Greenwich Mean Time. There's no springing forward to standard time or falling back to daylight-saving time, or Mountain time, or changing to this time or that time. In Togo there is just time, unchanging, as you change. Life in Togo is mostly lived outdoors, and it's easy there to get by without a watch. When the sun blues the horizon, it's 6 a.m. When the sun's a yellow eye glaring straight down from above, it's noon. When the sun flattens itself against the trees, turning the green horizon red, it's 6 p.m. When it gets dark, people go to the bistros and dance to tinkling highlife that melts into Bob Marley that melts into Bony M that melts into Michael Jackson that melts into Sunny Adé and into highlife again, and eventually melts into you and your Peace Corps friends. At your table you spread hot mustard on torn sections of baguette and wash it down with liter bottles of Bière Benin. You dance, you drink. You marvel at the straight-backed, full-breasted, firm-bottomed, ebony women, swaying hips wrapped in blazing-bright *pagnes* that wrap around your imagination. They marvel at you, at your white skin now clothed in African fabrics, familiar yet strange-looking because you're a stranger to this country no matter how you try to disguise that fact, dressed as you are in your sweaty African *bou-bou* cut open and deep at the sides to let in as much air around your chest and under your armpits as possible—your sweaty *bou-bou* made from some blinding Dutch-wax print of, say, brown seagull silhouettes set against an orange background with purple explosions outlined in yellow for good measure; you, standing or sitting there in your well-broken-in leather sandals—the first purchase you made during your first hesitant trip outside the safe haven of your hotel or the Peace Corps office in the capital city of Lomé, away from the group (but not too far away; you went with two or three other new volunteers, certainly someone who could speak a little French)—you in your sandals purchased for more than full price because you didn't know how to bargain, sandals so well molded to your feet you wonder why you ever wore shoes. Music. Bière. Sweat. Heat. And after a while, you and your restaurant French get up the courage to walk over and ask one of those lovely women to dance. She laughs at your carefully rehearsed sentence with its words lining up like ducks in a row, smiles no, and as you walk away, pretending it doesn't matter, she pulls your hand from behind and leads you onto the dance floor. And after a while, time is the last thing on your mind.

But old habits die hard, and you've never seen anything quite like it, so after the new African shirts and sandals, the watch becomes the next purchase for the well-heeled Peace Corps volunteer, circa 1982. Somewhere and somehow within this new family of yours, this family of new volunteers you met at pre-staging in a Philadelphia Marriott, your new family arc-welded together through a collective throwing of caution to the wind, soldered by risk; somewhere someone coined the term and it stuck: "Stevie" watches, and you had to have one because—because they were—well, funny. An artifact. A souvenir of your experience, of your time here in Togo. You go to party headquarters in the capital city, party headquarters of the one party allowed to exist here, led by Gnassingbe Eyadema, dictator in 1982 and now, 18 years later in 2000, as you think back in wonder at what you did and didn't do and know and didn't know and didn't choose to know. Stevie watch? The dictator's first name in French is Etienne, Stephen in English. Togo, your new home for two years, was first a German protectorate, then a French territory before it declared its independence in 1960. The first president, Sylvanus Olympio, by most accounts a good man from the southern Ewe tribe, most populous of the 21 ethnic groups that reside in this country, lasted two years before he was killed. In 1967 Eyadema, a lieutenant colonel from the northern Kabye tribe, led the coup that overthrew the next government. Uneducated yet cunning, the new president promotes his fellow Kabyes to positions of power and consolidates his rule over the small country. He studies his friend Sese Seko Mobutu of Zaire, a dictator ever clad in a leopard-skin cloak to remind people that's what he turns into if ever threatened, so don't. Eyadema learns the power of mystique, and the watch is all part of it. The watch is gold with a dark green face and a red-, yellow- and green-striped plastic band. The watch itself is a simple affair: the only digits the 12, 3, 6 and 9, with hatch marks in between. What makes it a Stevie watch is a head-and-shoulder photo of the stern Eyadema in full military regalia peering out from behind the hands, glaring out at you, the wearer. The sweep hand sits on the edge of an optic disk that makes the face appear and disappear every 20 seconds. The message: Stevie is watching, all the time, whether you see him or not. To you the watch seems funny, a keepsake of your two years doing "the toughest job you'll ever love." During in-country cross-culture training you were told not to talk politics in Togo; you never know who might be listening, and you might get someone in trouble. So you wear your watch with glib abandon; to your unpracticed eyes, the country, by African standards, seems robust and healthy. Your Togolese friends tolerate your naiveté when they spot the watch, manage a hesitant smile, click their tongues and go "Hmmm, hmmm, hmmm." You are their guest. You are there to help. You are from America.

So you buy the watch but not the comic book. Somehow— somehow the comic book goes too far, this comic book hawked by Lomé children while you eat your lunch of rice with peanut sauce in an open-air café. Children without sandals, in dusty shorts and thin, sweaty, seam-popping, Chinese-made T-shirts approach your table with a small stack of Gnassingbe Eyadema comic books drawn in muscular, Spiderman-like animation. French text balloons with lots of exclamation marks float above a soldier with clear, purposeful eyes and bulging forearms destined for an iron grip. You don't buy one, but through the grapevine you know which page to flip to as you feign interest to the eager Togolese child: It shows in fiery color the plane crash of 1974 in the village of Sarakawa. A monument featuring the wreckage has been built at the crash site. An entire spread is devoted to the "Miracle of Sarakawa": The now-president walks away from the broken fuselage that was flying him up country to his tribal home in the North. The dazed, bleeding but tremendously muscular Kabye leader in military garb staggers from the smoking wreckage. Cradling an injured arm, he gazes straight at the reader and says, *"Je vie…ENCORE!"* (I live…STILL!). Through your blissful 25-year-old eyes—eyes that out of habit check the time on your Stevie watch, sometimes just to watch his visage appear fully for 20 seconds and then slowly disappear, sometimes just to laugh because it's so silly, so Third World—life in Togo seems all right. Sure, people are poor, but they're making it. Your middle-class Togolese teacher friends seem pretty comfortable. Just don't talk politics. Just don't talk politics. You'll get them in trouble if you do. So you don't. Because you really don't want to know, anyway.

The family that lives closest to you, the Adades, has an assignment: Take care of the American. He is the guest of the village, and some-one must be able to get to him quickly in case of trouble: a snake or scorpion in the house or on the porch, or if he falls ill to any number of the maladies that seem to strike these Americans without warning. Any family in the village would be proud to fulfill this role, but because of simple geography, and because Monsieur Adade is an important and respected farmer, the village elders have bestowed upon him and his family this honor. Every new Peace Corps volunteer has an imme-diate assignment as well: From the many young Africans who come to help you unpack, choose the one who will clean your house and do your laundry during your stay. In Peace Corps parlance, this lucky teen-ager becomes your "kid." It is a coveted job because of what it is: a job, working for an American. And as everybody knows, Americans have money. "But once you hire a kid, it's awfully hard to change your mind," you are advised in training. "Choose carefully. Take your time." Because you are male, teen-age boys come to ask for the job: clear-eyed, earnest boys, all with good references. Whom to choose? You dither away another weekend, thinking. Then Monday, after teach-ing, you motor home on your mo-ped and the decision has been made for you: Akossiwa, Papa Adade's 15-year-old daughter, has already swept your porch and is waiting patiently to be let inside with her bucket, broom and rags. Smart girl. A strong-looking girl with a shy smile. Not too pretty. Something tells you that this is a good thing. She offers to come twice a week during *sieste* to clean, do the dishes, wash the floors, take home laundry and leave you with the African sound bite you will forever associate with this time, this place: the swoosh of her hand broom whisking the packed dirt in front of your house into overlapping seashell shapes as she leaves. The sound tugs you gently out of *sieste* and becomes the centerpiece of your post-nap ritual: raiding your kerosene-powered *frigo* for the never-too-empty carafe of sun tea, slipping out onto your porch and easing back to reality with a sugary, cool glass of Lipton's. You sit still in the creaky wicker chair, gazing down at the pretty seashells on seashells on seashells, sculpted by a tired but giggly girl who just thought dirt would look nice that way. And every time you're ready to leave, to return to school or shop for supplies, you pause on the porch before stepping down and ruining such temporal perfection. Yes, Akossiwa was a good choice.

And at night, if you are late and your little house sits there dark, the Adade family wonders where you are and worries. In the blackness Papa Adade will walk over with his lantern in one hand and something else in his other. On your porch he will place a little oil lamp made from cut and soldered tomato and sardine cans, light the rag wick, set the flickering yellow beacon at the spot most visible from afar, and leave.

There are no good snakes in Togo. It is halfway through the school day, the school day that begins at 6:45 with the raising of the flag in the dusty courtyard, the courtyard graced at the beginning of the school year with lovely shade trees, now stubby amputees, branches hacked back mercilessly by students with machetes in defense against snakes. The low, cement, barracks-like classrooms seem all window frame: huge, square, glassless cavities that pray for wind. The flag, wide green-and-yellow stripes, red square in the corner, one white star inside the red square. The singing of the national anthem in French. All students neat and crisp in their uniforms, boys in khaki trousers and shirts, girls in knee-length khaki skirts and white blouses. All students stand at attention in their classes and sing softly, words slurring together from the boredom of repetition, soft and familiar, like the gentle green morning, a warm but comfortable 80 degrees that's already climbing. School will end at noon when the temperature closes in on 100. From noon to 3 the country sleeps in a communal *sieste*. After 3, many kids return for an hour or two of work, maintaining the school garden or clearing more ground in defense against snakes. But now it is 9:45, between periods three and four, break time, time to eat, and the women from the village have arrived and set up their food stands: Big, wide, red, white, yellow and blue enamel bowls from China sit atop squat wooden tables, the biggest bowls for rice, the smaller bowls for tomato sauce with sardines, strips of fried dough rolled in sugar, half-ears of roasted corn served on torn pieces of brown sack paper, oily noodle and couscous concoctions, noodles and rice served on split baguettes, fried turkey tails. A bowl to keep the loose change in. The paper money disappears quickly somewhere in the folds of their bright *pagnes*. The women sit in what shade the courtyard trees provide; the students cluster under what other shade is offered by the roof and sides of the classroom buildings. There is a laughing, murmuring; there is the heat of the midmorning sun. The teachers visit under the best shade tree, reserved just for them, the village's upper-middle class. Ten minutes to go until fourth period. A girl points and screams.

"Serpent!"

Bowls fall. Bodies rush. Dust rises. A circle forms. Stones, sticks, books, a brick, bowls, bigger stones, more stones, stones stones stones rain down on the twisting black thing that looks even more lethal as it coils and flips, its underside soft gray and obscene in the daylight. A teacher runs to the office and returns with a machete. With a sure stroke he decapitates the viper, then works the blade under the middle of the headless now-non-danger, balances the limp body curled in the shape of an *N*, and marches it off to toss into the brush. Everyone filters back to their places in the shade. The student-body president rings the school bell. The market women pack up and walk home together, raising the dust on the path as they go. The courtyard empties. Fourth period begins. You wouldn't want to be a snake in Togo.

But you may want to be a crazy person. At first it's a curiosity, then a suspicion, then a certainty. Your friend Tom, math teacher from Michigan in the next village down the road, notices it one day out of the blue: In every village there's a crazy person, sometimes two. They show up on market day, at the taxi stop, at your front doorstep if it happens to be your village. They seem to materialize everywhere you want to be. Crazy people dressed in tatters with a second, third, fourth skin of dust and grime, some not dressed at all; crazy people with missing teeth and the glaring, faraway look in their eyes, the look that makes them crazy people. But there's the other thing: They never lack for food or drink. They're never angry. Just crazy. Nice crazy, if there is such a thing. The market women leave them what remains at day's end; the villagers leave an old sheet outside their huts. The villagers don't seem to care if a crazy person sleeps under their awning at night or inside the mud-and-thatch tool shed. They don't care if a crazy person is the first thing they see when they step outside in the morning.

"The village takes care of them," your African friend the histo-geo teacher says at the taxi stop after school. You're both heading into Atakpame on Friday night. He is dressed in a crisply pressed aqua-marine *complèt* peppered with orange lightbulbs inside of which leap purple sailfish. He looks great. You wonder why these clothes never look half as good on you. That evening your paths might cross in town as you bistro-hop and highlife dance through the thick night air. A crazy man dressed in a yellow-and-green Bob Marley T-shirt and nothing else capers around the taxi *gare*, tries to help the driver lash the luggage down on top of his pickup; the driver shoos him away. The crazy's dusty penis flops this way and that. The women climb on board, laughing and tittering in Ewe.

"In America we put them somewhere," you say, climbing up and settling into the seat across from the histo-geo teacher. "In these places just for them."

He shrugs. "We have one of those places, too. In Aného. But there are so many—" Together you watch how the villagers acknowledge the crazy man, make room for him. "Do you think they are happy in those places?" he asks.

You shrug.

All which prompts Tom, after the fourth or fifth *bière* at 2 a.m. inside the swirl, sway and sweat of that bistro night, to say something silly and drunken and a little profound: "Yeah. When I've had it with America, with Reagan, with everything—" (and we all know just what he means, because having had it with America helped push us here) "when I've had it with everything, I'll buy me a one-way ticket back. And when I get here I'll throw off all my clothes and become a *fou* in Togo. That's what I'll do." And we all get back up and dance like fools.

This here, this here heat is mirage heat. This here heat is a mother, a user, using you like a lightning rod to reach the earth, then cooking its way back up through your feet, your calves, thighs, crotch, belly, chest, armpits, neck, face and back out the top of your head and through the hat that seems to make no difference. This heat, you are this heat, a human ripple rising through the trunks, leaves and vines of this rain-forest country, country fried by sun into your retinas, an impossible electric green green that out-neons neon. Heat. Heat like the buzz of mosquitoes that never stops, the buzz and bite you keep out with your mosquito net like a winding sheet that makes it even hotter inside on your damp bed, lying naked there with your lover, still, separate, arms limp, palms up, legs spread-eagled, the two of you a feast for the one mosquito that always makes it in to remind that you can run, you can hide, but you can never get away from this heat.

Until it rains. Cat-fur-gray mountains of mist drift over the peaks of Ghana, gathering, gathering, gathering gobs of gray greatness: slate gray, ocean gray, gauzy gray, purgatory gray, waiting gray, charcoal gray, black! The clouds pile one atop the other atop another to over-whelm the sun, to turn midday into dusk, to snuff out the heat like a lantern run out of fuel. The first falling drops silver the forest green to blue, raising dust-cloud explosions from the packed earth. Drop, drop-drop, drop-drop-drop; the drops clack and thunk against the corrugated steel roof of your little house. But only for a second. Then Africa's tiger god tears through the clouds with a mighty claw, and water falls, water weeps. It is more than rain that pours down from on high; it is the definition of rain that slams down from above, slaps down on the corrugated steel roof over your head and snaps the heat in two. Thunderous, wondrous the sound, the sound of the heavens raining down on the steel roof, forming rushing parallel rivers that fall and pound the ground with spatter. You and your African lover lie awake under the net, inside and within the cool roar; she slaps at the mosquito that's landed on your belly, gets it. A smear of blood, the glow of waiting skin in the gray room, white-white, black-black, white-black, skin is skin is desire under the pelting rain and cool mercy and you're at it, rocking together as the rain rocks the roof, the house, rocks your world louder than your love that furrows and sweats these dank sheets. You scream, she screams, you scream your hearts out. Who can hear? Scream as loud as you like; you cannot out-passion this rain.

After 20 minutes it is over. Like a beaten bully back with reinforcements the sun slogs through the breaking, spent clouds, steaming the ground, and already there are dry spots surfacing in this in-between gray-green-and-brown-dripping world. A moment: a still moment, and you and your lover venture outside, pull together two wicker porch chairs and open a bottle of *bière* to share as you wait for the next moment, which comes... wait... which comes... wait... there's one; there's another... which comes... Now! Suddenly the air is aflicker-flutter with amber wings, thousands of lacy wings, twittering, tapping, throbbing the air like a pulse: tremble. Termites! Hatched by the rain, up through the soil, dried by the air: termites. Wings by the thousands, lace wings blurring your vision, up, down inways-sideways-out, then falling, filtering gentle down to earth, little brown bodies with Tinkerbell wings, gliding back to earth. Enter... toads! Toads big as your hand spread wide, toads emerging with a swagger from the slick, dripping forest. Toads with tongues long, quick and obscene, tongues that lap, lap, lap up eight or nine scurrying termites at a swoop. The ground glitters with shiny termite bodies, scattering, fast. Three toads sit and spit out their tongues, flop, flop, flop, feasting. You've heard that the Togolese eat the termites too, fry them up in a pan, salt them, toss them back like popcorn. You turn to your Togolese lover to ask if this is true, but she is sipping your shared *bière*, laughing with you at nature's spectacle, looking beautiful and whole. You turn back, ashamed of some of the things you find yourself thinking about these people, some of the things you laugh about when you're alone with your Peace Corps friends, the Peace Corps urban legends you buy into. And what if it is true? You got a better use for termites? Brightness: The sun has broken all the way through, tanning the drying earth; fewer termites and toads, fewer, and soon it will be as dusty, hot and still as before.

There's no escaping it because the children are everywhere: tagging along behind on the street, on the way at the *marché*, even calling through the open windows of the bistros. The *yovo* song: "*Yovo, yovo, bonsoir. Ça va bien? Merci!*" When asked, the adults shake their heads and tell you *yovo*, in Ewe, translates as "one who is free because of his intelligence." They deny the Peace Corps rumor that what it really means is *yellow dog*, which is how it feels after the 20th time kids aim it at you on any given day. You will never belong here. You may think your skin is black because black skin is mostly what you see. You forget what color you are. But the children are fine-tuned to other-ness, alien-ness, to the French you work so hard to speak better that's never good enough. "*Yovo, yovo, bonsoir. Ça va bien? Merci!*" In groups, alone, you swear you even heard it through the open window of your house while drowsing through *sieste*. Some kid singing it to himself as he walked down the path by your house. Story: One time a Peace Corps volunteer was walking along the main drag in Atakpame, you know, the busy street that curls like a bow around the grand *marché* building? Bunch of Togolese kids was trailing him, *yovo*-ing him. It was noon. It was hot. You know how hot I mean: headache hot. He snaps, whirls around to tell them to fuck off. The kids scatter, one into the road, right in front of a taxi that almost runs him over. Could have killed him. How'd you like to carry that around with you the rest of your life? Just ignore 'em. Keep walking. What else can you do? "*Yovo, yovo, bonsoir. Ça va bien? Merci!*"

The school year begins with 60 students per class. They sit on benches, two to a desk. When you walk in, the class major claps his desktop and everyone stands at attention until you tell them—or wave your hand—that it is all right to sit down while you take attendance. Nice, such respect. This isn't America, you think. No, it's not, which is why most students here flunk and flunk and flunk again until they eventually drop out. The class is the equivalent of ninth grade. Ages range from 13 to 18. Only the best pass the final examinations that eventually promote them to *lycée*, where many of the rest flunk out. What use has a country like Togo for a well-educated population, a population that can't find jobs? No use. Negative use; what dictator wants an educated class of people who read too much, a class of people who ask too many questions that have no good answers? No use.

But the American is nice, and silly in a way we have not seen. Without warning, in the middle of class, he starts to jump up and down. "I am jumping," he says. And he pulls up a student or two from their desks, makes everyone get up and jump about the room. "We are jumping," he says. We jump, bump into one another, bump into him, laugh. And he points to me: "And what is Manavi doing? She is —she is—" and he looks around at us until Kudjo gets it: "Manavi laughs. Manavi is laughing," he grins.

"Yes!" teacher says. "We laugh when we learn English," and then we sit when he waves us back down. "We jump*ed*," he says, to teach past tense. "And what *will* we do tomorrow?" He grins.

"We will jump. We shall jump!" we answer. But even though we pass this class and Monsieur Kuevi's science class and Madame Ekoue's French class, the test will come from the capital, and we will go only so far. We miss too much school. We have work in the fields. I must help my mother in the market. This first, that second, then school. And by mid-year our number has dropped to 45, then 40. And the school year will end and the jumping Peace Corps man will leave, and next year we will be here again, maybe next level, maybe not; and again, until we finally flunk the test many times and we don't bother to come anymore.

Buzzards perched on the awning of the Badou meat market, eight black question marks, then six; two of the 20-pound birds break rank, descend and fight on the ground, their red, bald heads connected by a piece of gristle stretched to the breaking point. A tug of war. They flap 3-foot black wings at each other and twirl in the dust, a whirligig, yellow sun glinting off their backs, dust rising. For some reason God has seen fit to sear this image into your memory. You've seen buzzards before, in other *marchés*, other meat markets. But, watching, you know that this scene, this moment in the Badou *marché*—you glance at the position of the sun, the slant of shadows on the ground; it's about 3 in the afternoon—this moment on this Saturday, pausing here in the shade while your friend Brian buys soap and sardines from the mother of one of his students, this non-moment, devoid of any importance; Brian, who teaches math/science, whom you've traveled four long hours in the back of a Toyota pickup to visit on this Saturday in the middle of your two years because the Chloroquine-induced dreams you've been having grow more and more bizarre: In the last one the green jungle crept up and over your house at night while you slept, and in the morning you were not there, your house was not there; just jungle that swallowed you up; all very vivid, like the tribal-language babble of

103

the market; the slam of a tailgate at the neighboring taxi station, the cry of a baby girl clinging to her mother's leg, the heat streaming down to bake it all in your memory, the vectors of vision meeting at the gaggle of buzzards lining the top of the Badou meat market: This moment will remember you. The blood-red cleavers chopping the bloodier red meat below; the bloody red fingers of the butchers tossing a scrap into the dust now and then and the buzzards falling. It's not a good memory; it's not a bad memory. It just is. Brian zips up his backpack and tugs your sleeve. "C'mon. Let's get a *bière*," and the trance is broken, but the memory is branded and will remain.

Everything grows here. Lily-like amaryllis, trumpety blooms open and loud in scarlet, pink and white. Flamboyants in searing orange and yellow, tendrilly stamens curled like inviting fingers. Bougainvillea spreading up the white-washed sides of an old German two-story, a crimson supernova! Caladium, leaves large as elephant ears, veiny rosy-red stitched around the edges laced with slips of white-speckled green. Nerine blooms, pink, huge and spidery! Hibiscus in creamy butter-scotch and orange, crinkly, papery; bushy lantana, thousands of red-yellow-orange blooms the size of diamonds. Oleander, shrubby, waxy, pink, white, red! Ribbony red-yellow Rothschild lilies, pasted like Christmas bows against palm tree trunks. Jasmine, honeysuckle, birds of paradise. Yes, birds of paradise all in this Jack-and-the-beanstalk world.

Perhaps every place on earth has its own God. That is to say, when one place stops being that place and starts being another place, the god in charge changes, changes to suit the new place. That would mean there were many gods on which to conjecture. But no one would doubt or conjecture as to the god in charge of Togo, West Africa: She is a woman, a naked woman bedecked in flowers, with green eyes.

It is late afternoon and starting to cool. The first squadrons of fruit bats fly overhead, southbound: black, silent bombers peppering the blue-pink sky.

The road runs north-south, splitting the country into neat east-west halves. Two lanes, paved but crumbling on the edges, it sometimes drops off on each side by as much as 8 inches. The road begins where the land does, in Lomé—the maritime region—then runs due north across the flatlands through Tsevie and Notse, then Atakpame, farther still through miles of drier and drier savannah through Blitta, Sotoboua, then Sokode, where men in Muslim white start to rival those in brilliant African clothes; still north the road courses through the dictator's tribal territory, Lama Kara and Pya, where he's built a second party headquarters but really a stronghold for him to escape to in case in case; next comes Niamtougou, Kanté, Mango and finally, after Dapaong, the border crossing into Burkina Faso, where stunted, lonely trees speckle the brown-paper flatness, providing far too little shade. Think back to Sokode, dry Sokode: There the paved road makes a *T*, the western arm stretching off to Bassar near the Ghanaian border, the eastern arm snaking off to Tchamba, cozy close to Benin. Lower down, in Atakpame, the paved road branches west in a long, lazy loop, taking in the large town of Kpalime before returning home to Lomé. The eroding two-lane is called the Route Internationale. In America it would be represented by a thin blue line on the map, a county road.

Soon you know the country inside out, up-down and side-to-side, by the villages where your friends are posted. "You know the country better than we do," your Togolese friends laugh as they settle in beside you in the back of a *baché*: converted Toyota, Nissan and Mitsubishi pickups that endlessly travel the Route Internationale, crisscrossing the land, their truck beds lined with a bench on each side, covered with wooden canopies, overloaded with suitcases, boxes, baskets, pails, chickens and perhaps a goat strapped down up top, and African men, women with babies, boys, girls, and you below, inside, sitting thigh to thigh, sweating. The drivers all know each other by the wooden plaques mounted and centered above the cabs: "Not Yet" says one in red letters outlined in gold, the head of Jesus peering over the words from behind; "Which Way?" poses another in blue and orange, with one finger pointing up, another pointing down; "Why Not?" asks an old Datsun still running on one leg, a lone candle standing mysteriously between the two words. Heather, the English teacher from Malibu, lives in Wahala, the village plagued by guinea worm; Bret, from Syracuse, in Co-ops, works at the tractor place in Hiheatro; William, in Animal Traction, from Tucson, lives in Bafilo now and goes by the name of Bafilo Bill; math/science teacher Jim, from El Paso, with the Stetson hat, lives way north in Mango, where he needs it; Kristen, the health volunteer from San Diego, the one you had the crush on in training, loves out-of-the-way Kpagouda and still isn't interested in you; Abby and Lauren are neighbors up north in Kante, digging wells. You even know the whereabouts of the volunteers you don't like: Lyle, in pretty Elavagnon near the game park, who talks so much about leaving, you wish he'd just go; weird Wayne, the butterfly collector in Akaba; Frank in Guerinkouka, who only came over here to study for his GMATs; Dalton, the walker—where does he live again? Apeyeme?—doesn't matter; he's never there, always out walking. Good volunteers, bad volunteers, lonely volunteers all, trekking around this sliver of Africa in the back of pickups, on foot, astride Yamaha Enduros or Motobecane mo-peds, searching out someone like you to reconnect with, to talk it over and make it real.

"Yovo, yovo, bonsoir. Ça va bien? Merci!"

When there is nothing to do, a walk through the village will do. It is Saturday or Sunday. You're tired of reading, of writing letters home so you can get letters back (that most exciting moment of the day: to check the tiny window of your post-office box for those slanting lines of envelope edge). No one comes to visit; your papers are graded; the gardening is done, shopping, too. It is 1 o'clock in the afternoon. The village lies still under the spell of sun. You strike off at a diagonal, through the meandering, curling paths and squares between the clusters of mud huts with thatch roofs and little cement houses. Look sharp for all the sharp edges there are to confront a tall American: slanting awnings and roofs of corrugated steel that end 6 feet above the ground, right at eye level. Don't take any corner too quickly. A little boy starts to follow and is soon joined by one of his fellows. You don't hear "*yovo*" much in your own village anymore; mothers have scolded their children into silence. Still, the little ones like to follow. A naked baby girl, eyes squinted shut, stands soaped head to toe on a flat stone. Her mother pours a pail of water over her head. Faces peer through glassless windows; forms darken open doors as the village guest passes. Smiles mostly, bemusement, curiosity, nods of simple assent. And always a frown or two: Go ahead and look your fill. You get to leave anytime you want. We live here. You turn a corner into a private courtyard, a

U made by the connecting walls of three huts. A clothesline sags between the farthest points. A teen-age girl, bare breasted, hangs wrung-wrinkled laundry. She is halfway between the pile on the ground and the line with a crimson *pagne* when your eyes lock. A very pretty girl. Seventeen. Eighteen, maybe. Your student. "*Bonjour, Monsieur*," she smiles, and tosses the garment over the line, turning back so you can get a good look. *Take me with you*, say her eyes.

In December the winds increase in the drier North African nations of Algeria, Chad and Libya, picking up the top of the Sahara and blowing it southwest. For six weeks a country of airborne sand filters through the atmosphere between the sun and the Earth, painting gauzy, orange-muted sunrises and sunsets, separated by hours of twilight-looking days. Sand. Sand in the teeth of the comb. Sand under the fingernails. Sand up the nose, turning snot black. Sand in the ears. Sand like powdered snow on the louvers of window shutters. Sand that falls from the folds of clothing. Sand on the concrete floor no amount of sweeping can eliminate. The Africans, wrapped in layers, shiver in the 70-degree weather, but finally—save for the sand—finally, the American is comfortable.

In April the ending begins. Two years. Or has it been 20? Or two months? So slowly it went as you lived it; so quickly it goes as you remember it.

They come to your porch alone, with brothers and sisters, in small groups: students, friends, neighbors, teachers, clapping their hands outside your door and waiting for you to come so they can say goodbye.
Au revoir.
Farewell.
Goodbye: "Will you take our picture and send it to us?"
Au revoir. "Will you give me your backpack? Okay, then. May I buy it?"
Farewell: "Your gas stove and table; my wife, she—well, is it for sale? How much?"
Goodbye: "Can we be pen friends? May I have your address? Can you give my name to an American teen-ager?"

Au revoir. "Is the mo-ped yours, or does it belong to the *Corps de la Paix*? Oh."

Farewell: "You come, you stay as our guest, you teach our children, and once we start to care for you, you leave. Why? Why?"

Goodbye: Shy Akossiwa asks for nothing. She promises to clean one last time after you've gone, then realizes what this will be like and falls silent. To her you give a most sought-after item: your short-wave radio/cassette player, because every teen-age girl should have a radio to fall asleep to at night.

Au revoir. School is out for summer. The classrooms are vacant, the flagpole naked.

Farewell: Two years ago on this day you set foot in the country for the first time.

Goodbye.

Au revoir.

And the one who brought Africa into your bed at night, under the stars and rain, how do you say farewell to her?

Russell Tomlin *earned his M.F.A. at Mills College in Oakland. He served as a Peace Corps volunteer from 1981 to 1983 in Togo, West Africa, where he taught English as a foreign language. He is currently working on a collection of short stories.*

Bridges

Sarah Massey-Warren

Oh hunger that crosses the bridge between
                    —Susan Howe, "The Birth-mark"

Over the land over the land
I walked at morn
Singing and trembling with cold
                    —Southern Paiute, "A Morning Walk"

Prepare for misery," my client had said of the
spring weather before sending me to Elko, Nev., to research community life. She neglected to tell me that the people were among the
friendliest I would ever find. Small-town familiarity knits Elko's residents in communal warmth. Hospitality exceeds town boundaries; it
spills out to entice visitors and new residents to this unlikely hearth.
A booming economy stokes the hospitality. Elko boils with lucrative
work due to a recent low-grade gold-mining boom in nearby Carlin
and an indigenous tourist industry grown from legalized gambling.
The Red Lion Casino on the north side of town flies in three full
747s of eager gamblers to Elko's tiny airport daily.

An unexpected oasis in a state of desert and high plains wilderness, Elko is a late-blooming promised land. It draws emigrants from
California's urban sprawl and Colorado's uncertain economy. "Everybody and their dog are tired of taxes and expenses," declares Laura
Mandros, a chamber-of-commerce official. "We can't build hospitals
and schools fast enough. When Newmont Mining boomed in the
'80s, we had trailer parks and tons of new babies. They must have put
them in drawers."

A superficially sleepy community in which parents raise their children in relative safety, Elko's history bespeaks fast-paced economic growth that allows those in mining, grazing and gambling to change their futures from broke to hopeful almost overnight. Still, Elko defends its aura of extended family. "Most of us are homebodies," explains Laura. "Parents get involved in everything in this community. Everybody knows everybody." Except for the high-tech mining boom nearby, Elko remains warped into the '50s. Coffee here is never cappuccino; it's the regular java served with small-town warmth.

The Humboldt River parallels the town's boundary; two bridges straddle the current. Although Nevada records the lowest precipitation level in the United States, with an average of 6 inches per year, statistics seem irrelevant today at these particular bridges. Standing on the southern bridge looking north, I feel the insistent slivers of chill, wet wind penetrate eyes, skin, even clothing, like one-penny nails. Lamoille Canyon, just east of Elko, records the state high of up to 18 inches of precipitation annually, and today that drip shifts slantwise across this bridge.

It is early morning in late March of 1995. In dazed amazement at being here, I stare at the slate current churning underfoot. Although I am both a writer and a landscape architect with strong environmentalist leanings, I have accepted an assignment from a mining company to do nothing more than interview area residents. The contract pays unbelievably well. I am recently divorced, with sole custody of two daughters under 7 years of age and an astonishingly meager bank account. One foot in poverty, the other in my values, I straddle an uncertain economic future for my family. I consider this as thoughts of coffee draw my eyes to the Humboldt's northwestern shore, where the town's brick buildings huddle around Idaho Street, the historic main thoroughfare. Short and squat, with many of them built far before the turn of the century, the structures look like snowsuited children waiting to be called inside for hot chocolate when sent out to play in bitter weather. With a population of approximately 30,000, including its outlying suburbs, Elko hasn't many buildings.

Craving hot coffee, I linger on the bridge, inhaling this lucrative and contested terrain. The Ruby Mountains parallel the eastern shore. In the mist, they bunch into humped pachyderms. Once the sun clears, they metamorphose—exclamatory sculptures against pollution-free azure. Except near Reno and Las Vegas, Nevada's skies evade contamination. Beyond the Rubies stretch still more parallel mountain ridges. To the west, even more mountain chains—"an army of caterpillars" according to geologist C.E. Dutton—interspersed with valleys and high plateaus striate the state from border to border. More than 160 mountain ranges define some 90 drainage basins, which add up to the Great Basin.

Originally a self-contained land of interior river drainage, what is now Nevada first lured migrating Indian tribes and then a population of tough, independent Caucasians, all of whom nonetheless respected the physical terrain. The territory's first residents of European descent —miners, traders and farmers—followed the early explorations of John Fremont, Peter S. Ogden and Joseph Walker looking for land and a future that belonged solely to them. They formed an independent territorial government in the 1850s before the discovery of the Comstock lode in 1859. However, geology defined the people even as they attempted to define themselves. Ancient and unsettled soils and substrate with a history of uplift, faulting, flooding and drainage nurtured above-ground inhabitants. The restless rocks endowed early settlers with the country's richest mineral deposits: gold, silver, copper, manganese, tungsten and mercury. Once gold surfaced and shone from the Comstock area, the secret spilled over territorial lines. Any hope of quiet self-sufficiency splattered clear to Washington, D.C. Dropped into the national political sieve, Nevada blossomed from a territory in 1861 to a state in 1864, sought after for the taxes on its minerals, rights to its land, its anti-slavery status during the Civil War and its support of the Republican Party.

Although the ruling national political parties seesawed during the following decades, the struggle between the state and the federal governments over Nevada land escalated with entrenched heel-digging on both sides. Environmentalists upped the stakes with a romantic insistence on returning the land to a "natural" state, rescued from mining and grazing. Even Nevada rivers, which once siphoned into the state's interior basins, have since been partially dammed and drained to California.

Elko's residents work with the earth, relying on grazing and mining. As resident custodians and cultivators of the resources that benefit the federal government and neighboring states, as well as their own families, they resent the interference. The people embody the state's independent stance. According to Laura, my chamber-of-commerce informant, "The local attitude is, 'Leave us alone. Let us do our thing.'"

From the bridge, I notice the railroad tracks that parallel the Humboldt on the town's side of the river, recently moved there from the center of town. Transportation molded the town after 1859, when the Canadian Pacific Railway's system spidered nationwide, weaving a web of gold mines and cattle ranches. Now, Interstate 80 and the Elko Airport have preempted the tracks. Although destined to become a major copper-mining site around 1900, Elko's prominence on the transportation system in 1868 transformed it into a party town for herders. Over the weekend, cattle and sheep men would drink in the town's saloons and brawl over women in the adjacent brothels. Come Monday, they returned to fighting over grazing rights in the nearby valleys.

Gold and silver strikes in nearby Tuscarora in 1867 and extensive grazing acreage nurtured the nascent town and its unusual genetic mix. Chinese railroad workers moved to Elko when the completion of the Canadian Pacific system left laborers out of jobs. The Chinese immigrants planted the town's first gardens and established its water-supply system. In addition, the Canadian Pacific management cultivated a friendly relationship between Elko and another colorful contingent—the western Shoshone, Northern Paiute and Owyhee Indians—whose ancestors had arrived there 12,000 years before the white settlers. The railroad company gave each Indian chief free passenger status and allowed tribal members to ride without charge in the freight cars. Finally, in the late 1880s, Basques from the Pyrenees fleeing the fascism of General Franco immigrated to Elko. Joining the other sheepherders, they became major players in town development.

Adolescent Elko flourished, becoming the county seat and home to 2,000 individuals by March of 1869. Within five years, its residents built the brick county courthouse that remains today. More noticeably, the town residents concocted their complex and spicy character. Elko mixed traditional mining and grazing interests with an odd scramble of entertainment acts and family living. Booking big-name casino acts began here. Celebrities included Lawrence Welk, Sophie Tucker, the Dorsey Brothers, the Andrews Sisters, Chico Marx, and Bing Crosby, who was named honorary mayor. These days, the town hosts more legalized brothels than any city in the United States.

In many residents' view, these industries contribute economically to town life—good neighbors in a family community. The mining taxes and donations support schools, highways, police and youth activities. Newmont Mining subsidizes education in advanced technology, keeping the youth in town after high-school graduation and the average family income of $38,000 (1995) higher than anywhere else in the state. Appreciative of the land that feeds them, the cattle grazers initiate statewide conservation practices and legislation protecting the industry and, thus, town residents. Basque family money underlies much of the town's retail and restaurant base. Gambling income cancels the need for state taxes. Even prostitutes donate generously to community causes. If residents agree on nothing else, they insist that recent government and environmentalist interference is unwelcome and destructive to family life because it restricts income and eliminates jobs through stifling legislation.

Pausing on the bridge, I recognize the issues that straddle the people and their land. As a landscape architect, I think first of the needs of the land. A passionate walker, I welcome the first sunrise hours of every morning as I walk the land outside town. However, in the course of four days of interviews with miners, grazers and town residents, I keep seeing the people and their struggle to raise families and build futures. Theirs is the same struggle of any person trying to earn a living. In Elko, for my client's purposes, I am a writer and must make sense of these competing needs. The land, the people. The town, the federal government. The sides seem clear, but my perspective is not. I wonder, need this be polemical, or is there hope for some dialectical evolution beyond stalemate? Sooner or later, I have to leave the bridge and begin interviewing again. Despite the cold, I cuddle against the bridge's metallic railings. An odd aerie, this, an exposed perch that posits me precariously close to nature and people.

Only by "taking sides" from a removed vantage point off the bridge might I perceive the whole of stream and bridge. The "big picture," though, is an illusion. Perspective is a *chosen* view. Designers select perspective drawings, with their distorted scales stretched to reflect the architect's vision, as the persuasive graphic tool for convincing a client to buy into a plan. In perspective drawings, we vividly see what we are meant to see.

Life resonates with complex sensuality. We hunger, taste, hear voices of friends and songs of birds. We feel hot and cold, love and hate. Land layers below us in rock, above us in leaves, around us in wildlife, friends and family. No single perspective can encapsulate our lives anywhere, including in Elko.

On the bridge, I detach from all sides, suspended in judgment. I fish down from the arch and catch myself and the universe reflected back. This is the designer's cross section, in which an unbiased scale applies equally to people and nature. Water, stream, arch, memory and anticipation infuse me. All moments collapse into one, as horizontal path and hourly progressions snap. My spirit dissolves with spirits of place and people behind me and beyond. All melts into the bridge. As technicians, we bring the bridge to nature. Gazing into the reflective waters beneath, the bridge inescapably brings us back to ourselves and links us to "other"—organic, inorganic and political.

"The bridge does not happen without the stream beneath it," observes Jeffrey Robinson. He reflects on common images in English Romantic poetry that juxtaposed nature imagery with the industrial changes occurring simultaneously: "A bridge seems an animated path, we feel life and movement in the bridge itself. ... Suddenly the bridge is flooded with questions about human beings, questions that seem to erupt from no recognizable point in the bridge's history." In Elko, the landscape has changed, but the issues persist. The people need to work, the land needs to thrive, and the government seems to need to control this dynamic. The people—local, federal, environmental— and their overarching conflicts are nothing without the land. Bridge as metaphor, uniting disparate individuals in an overriding purpose. Bridge as metonymy, allowing separate interests to form connected but discrete identities. Which is it? Is this only a turf battle, or is some larger issue at stake? Do I have to choose one perspective, one side of the construct? It is time to leave the bridge and see the people. The bridge is not part of the assigned journey, but it floods my thoughts. With no answers, at least I do know where to find coffee, and I thoughtfully leave the arch's refuge.

People and Mining

The highway leading to Carlin humps over high plateaus and past the pillars of the Adobe Range. Victim pillars lean abruptly. The predator wind tears down from mountain ridges and sculpts whatever lies in its path. It gulps the land, rocks my car, howls victoriously and rushes on. Dutton's "caterpillars" guard arid spaces and protean plateaus, all shifting with the vehicle's rapid progression. Stunned by the unusual beauty, I can barely keep my eyes on the road. However, I must. Heavy trucks hauling ore and mining products have reshaped the pavement as dramatically as the wind remodels the landscape. I stop four times between Elko and Carlin, thinking that my rented vehicle has four flat tires.

Ten miles outside Carlin, the monolithic mine structures erupt. The mustang road bucks more abruptly; the landscape melts to moonscape. Nature and man conspired here to create feelings of awe and trepidation of the pure power of the mining operation and the inconceivable wealth lying beneath the surface.

Generally, visitors cannot enter Newmont Mine. However, my client has arranged for me to spend the day touring the facility. Many of Elko's and Carlin's residents have worked at the mine since the company bought the TS Ranch, which included the old Carlin Mine, in the 1960s. Newmont milked the Carlin trend and developed state-of-the-art technology for leaching low-grade ore. Booms resounded in the mid-'80s with the improvement of the technology and the opening of plants two and five. Now, hyperscaled structures defy measure—roasters, mills, even mammoth garages housing two-story trucks larger than my house. Quarries within the mine move hundreds of thousands of tons of dirt each day. Everything surrounding me is on a scale so incomprehensible that I find it far easier to focus on the human faces explaining all of this to me.

Bob Harris, the mobile maintenance supervisor, looms over me like the mining structures, a smiling giant with broad shoulders and weather-beaten face. Twenty-seven years ago, he started as a quarry worker. Mining, he says, pays better than any other area job and offers far more opportunities for education. Much has metamorphosed since he first came to Newmont. Ranks of colleagues multiplied from 175 to 2,050. Technical changes shot Newmont from a mine that merely blasted or panned to one that could process tons of waste ore in hours. In the early 1970s, the company developed the heap leaching process. Before this, waste material was siphoned into the rotating cylinders of ball mills. Rock and a water solution were added and ground to a slurry. The mixture was pumped into leach tanks, followed by carbon. Now, plastic shrink-wraps slopes of material once believed to be "waste." Mountains of crushed rock are piled on top and sprinkled with a cyanide solution, leaching the gold onto the plastic. The sprinklers remind me of irrigation systems for growing perennials. Here, they cultivate gold. Four times cheaper than milling, the process allows Newmont to treat refractory ores containing sulfites or organic carbons, "turning gold into rock," grins Bob, by collecting the gold onto hardened carbon clusters.

"A war is being waged here because of the federal land issue," Bob says, echoing Laura. "Nevada is contesting the government. Only one-tenth of 1 percent of the ground surface in the state is disturbed by mining. Nevada was brought into the Union for mining in the 1860s. Now the government is reversing its position." He refers to what he sees as prohibitive taxes on mining products and equipment, which undermine the industry's ability to fund community schools, educational activities and youth programs. While acknowledging the necessity of environmental legislation designed to control the spilling of the chemicals used for leaching and blasting into underground water, he appears skeptical of the laws' severity. Silently, I accept his dismay. I do not tell him that as a landscape architect, I have had to help reclamation projects and address resource pollution. Bob's and others' stories of improved family lives with the advent of Newmont continue to dilute my rabid '70s environmentalism, although my love and respect for the land remain intact. I am continually reminded that people here work intimately with the land, while many environmentalists I know spend most of their time on computers and in meetings.

Kent Ames, who oversees truck and vehicle operations, takes me in hand for a tour of the south area of the quarry. *Truck* here does not resemble anything I conceive of as truck. These two-story, mechanical monsters have big feet. In order to drive, the operators climb 18 feet on external ladders, past 12-foot wheels. Their vehicles haul 190 tons of fill in each load, burn 25 gallons of diesel fuel an hour, and can drive only 36 miles per hour. Made by Caterpillar, these 54-foot-long behemoths weigh 428,000 pounds. I think of my economy Eagle Summit hatch-back in Colorado and wonder what it would look like under one of those tires.

To the tune of Kent's laughter, I scale a "truck" to ride with Thelma, the operator. Part Paiute, part Basque, this tiny grandmother less than 5 feet tall pilots the world's largest truck. Recognizing more money in the mines than she earned as a nurse, she had learned to drive 12 years prior. "The attitude toward women really changed since I started here. Back then, men treated you like dirt, expected you to lie down so they could walk over you like some carpet. Then they saw that women were operating the equipment just as good as them, so now we're equals, just friends." She waves to passing drivers as we talk and observes wryly, "'Course, men are men and women are women, and there's always going to be different ways of communicating. But it's better than it used to be."

Thelma's move to mining came at great cost. Her tribe disowned her, and she aches with the loss of her heritage. Still, she sees her kin as people with "lots of drinking problems who would rather live on government money because they don't know no better. I'm showing my kids a different way. They're all working and going to college."

Comparing child-rearing notes, we watch another monster dump its load. I peer over the sheer drop that parallels the road. "We have to drive on the left for better visibility," grins nonchalant Thelma as I gasp. The minicomputer screen over Thelma's head directs her to her own unloading site. As I leave the truck, what I saw as my challeng-ing single-parenting in Boulder diminishes into the prosaic.

Anchored to the earth, huddling in my jacket against the raging wind, I return to Kent. The quarry edge on which we stand rims a lay-ered hole hundreds of feet deep—driving down to Hades. We watch a blast. Again, my vocabulary quarry-warps. Every Tuesday and Thurs-day afternoon, *blast* here connotes multicolored columns of dirt, earth rainbows, shooting hundreds of feed skyward. "It's quite an art," Kent tells me. "College-trained technicians set different patterns for differ-ent breakage of the rock. It's done by remote control. The blaster and the powder man lay the pattern and turn a key that activates the battery. There is a five-and-a-half-minute lag time, then five numbers are keyed into the remote control, another lag time, then a sixth number, and the blast goes off. Only one person knows the sequence of numbers, which changes each day." Newmont not only metamorphoses dirt into aerial mountains but also turns the entire event into a company picnic. Families pick a vantage point and watch the earth blow up.

Leaving the bitter blasts of wind, I gratefully re-enter office space to meet with Mary Korpi, Newmont's articulate spokesperson for the Women's Mining Coalition. With a degree in chemical engineering, Mary joined Newmont 19 years ago and moved to the Carlin mine in 1987. She hungers for challenge. "There's more high tech here, more training and developing people. When I first came here, you got 10 warm bodies. Now we have experienced, committed workers." Echoing Kent, Mary resents the attitude that "people in mining are hired from the neck down." Although the coalition began as "a very idealistic movement," Mary describes it as "a highly organized working effort with a coalition of women from many mining companies. We educate freshmen senators that we're not a pick-and-shovel industry. The emphasis is on education. Miners are environmentally oriented people who fish and hunt every weekend like everybody else and love the outdoors." I quietly wonder how Thoreau, who regarded hunting and fishing as "every New England boy's" province, would respond to an educated group of women discussing hunting and fishing.

Women bring a sixth sense to mining and an appeal to home. The coalition devised a dollhouse display showing items, such as baby powder, adjacent to the rocks from which they were derived. It's all there —the linoleum on the floors, the Sheetrock in the walls, the computer chips, the microwave, makeup, cleansers—home sweet home, straight from the quarries. Science teachers receive rock samples related to household use for classroom purposes. "Where do they think they get this stuff?" Mary demands.

Women and community profit from mining. "When I started, there were very few women," Mary explains. "Now they say there's about 30 percent, but it's very biased, as those numbers come from the clerical pool. There isn't anybody in senior operational management. I hope it comes in my lifetime. Women are being hired as lawyers, though. Before, women had to work three jobs. Now, they're getting paid; they pay taxes; they go to college. They have a very valuable trade. Mining is a vital, active part of the community. Newmont's scholarship program for dependents of employees provides up to full room and board at colleges. Newmont makes a lot of donations to various sectors of money, equipment and trees. They sponsored the Handicapped Fishing Derby and the Big Orv playground. It's not done for attention or for an article in the paper, but because people want to do it."

"People" want to do it. "People" have more opportunities. The refrain returns with rhythmic insistence. "People" are living on this land, have been since the first Indian tribes crossed Nevada 12,000 years ago. Working "people here" are at odds with "people out there" in the legislature and in environmental movements. Rhetoric reverberates. I am dizzy with it all. The quarries inflict dismaying damage to the land. Yet these people stand before me; their needs reflect my own as a mother supporting daughters.

I recall "Sophie's Choice," but at least I have more time to choose. Leaving Newmont, I look for older voices. First I stop at the bridge and feel my head clear. The murky water gurgles. No reflection, mine or the universe's. Only the bridge casts a shadow.

Next to the bridge, I find Marj-n-Al's Mining Supply, owned by the Tussing couple. Al Tussing devoted 30 years to prospecting and spent 10 with mining companies. Eagerly he shows me a pan he used for harvesting gold and mercury from streams, tracing its dents and scratches. Picking up mineral samples and tools, he cradles each one in hands as rugged as the landscape surrounding Carlin. His voice hums, soft and enthused. He caresses each word. Relaxing, I lean into his lyric.

Prospecting requires mind and muscle, he says. "When I first started, I didn't know a dang thing about it. The first trip out, I hired a backhoe and said, 'Dig here, dig there.' Found nothing. So I read a lot of books, took a lot of courses, and learned to identify rocks correctly. Up until a few years ago, you could do a mineral homestead. It was the same as claiming 160 acres of land in Oklahoma. There, you built a house, improved the land, and got the land for a ridiculously low fee. Here, you put stakes right on the land; you got the rights to a mineral, not the land. You had to work to prove that a reasonable man could get a profit. To keep a patent, you had to keep the assessment work up and develop the property. This allowed somebody like me to stake a claim." Working first with a consortium of friends and then with his partner, Al sought uranium. "Prospectors were encouraged by the government to look for uranium. Now you have to pay

$100 a claim to the Bureau of Land Management. The government wanted to raise money for itself and actually lost it by knocking all the small individuals out of prospecting. They raised royalties from 2 to 8 percent. A lot of Nevadans still consider Nevada to be public lands. The BLM thinks it owns it."

Al left prospecting inadvertently. He sought the perfect mercury pan and only unearthed it by starting a store—with an unexpected price. "I meet a lot of people, get new play-toys, and have no time to prospect. I have to see what other people found," he chuckles. He insists that I contact John Alla, a "real prospector and businessman" who "has made and lost millions" prospecting. He scratches John's telephone number on a paper shred torn from a receipt; he is not the kind of business owner to keep letterhead memo paper. As I leave, he is smiling and fondling rocks.

Thursday morning, I wind through suburban streets lined with small homes and well-kept lawns. Tips of bulbs poke up from flower beds surrounded by gravel, though nothing blooms yet. Proserpine lurking among the rocks—why not? I park the car at John Alla's address, a modest, ranch-style house. At the door, a big, bald man with a shotgun travels tandem with the largest boxer I have ever seen. Right house, wrong reception. Gulping, I whisper my name to the concrete porch and turn around. "Come in," Big Man says to my back. His voice sounds gentle, like Al's, so I risk it. The screen door is open, the shotgun relaxed, pointed groundward, the dog already halfway out the door and sniffing my hand. "Just wanted to make sure you weren't from the government," he says. "Want a cup of coffee?"

We sit in a tiny kitchen around the small table—John, Buster (who keeps licking my hand) and me—as 78-year-old John talks. He waxes grandfatherly, pats the dog, refills my coffee cup, tells jokes. I wonder what happened to the guy who answered the door. "I hate the government," he explains, redundantly. "They've been trying to get my money, my claims, my equipment for years. I deceased myself in 1982. No more taxes. I have a good life, three grandchildren. Everybody should have as good a life as mine."

Working first for Barrick Mining in Utah in 1939, John served in the war, then returned to the mines. "I've been 42 years underground," he recalls. "It's nice. It don't rain. I liked the graveyard shift. There's nobody breathing down your neck. You could come out in the morning, get drunk, go back to work. I started prospecting in '82. I've made three or four fortunes—lead, silver, then a lot on barite. Lost a lot, too. Never go prospecting until you can afford it."

John seems a balanced guy. Hate for the federal government ("You sure you aren't from the IRS?") matches loathing for environmentalists. Both curtailed his own mining operations on more than one occasion. "Go to these environmentalists. Take their water, take their car, turn out the light. See how they like living without mining. Me and the BLM don't get along. North of Wells, when we were mining barite in '79, five guys from the BLM were stuck out there in the snow, snapping pictures. I made them walk. They said, 'Boy, am I glad to see you,' and I said, 'I'm not so sure you are.' They said, 'You aren't going to push us out?' and I said, 'No way! Push your own snow.' They said, 'You got no heart.' Hell, they had no heart when they shut me down! So I made them walk 10 miles back through the snow."

Humor and money remain intact and untracked. Many thousands of John's dollars lie in "Post Hole Savings and Loan." Once a heavy drinker, John quit alcohol 30 years back and now enjoys meeting friends like Al Tussing for coffee. He escorts me to the door, without the shotgun. "Come back next time you're in town," he waves, dog by his side. "But only if you're not with the government."

People and Grazing

Like community bedrock, mining grounds and subsidizes Elko's activities, college tuition, roads and playground equipment. Its organic counterpart is ranching, one of Elko's traditional meal tickets, its first Thanksgiving. The indigenous muse sings each January at the national Cowboy Poetry Gathering held in Elko. Standing on the bridge in the early morning, I remember that I have not eaten meat for 20 years. Still, looking at my reflection in the moving water, I appear diffused, broken up, fractal prisms of once-entrenched thinking. I accept what I see and move into my day.

By the time I visit Norm Glaser, a cattle rancher and former state senator, the cold, wet weather has lifted from Elko and drifted elsewhere. I drive through rolling ranchlands that parallel the Ruby Mountains, heading northeast toward Halleck. It is a chamber-of-commerce day; the light bounces off the stunning Rubies and sparkles in the Humboldt River at their base, and I find myself again falling in love with the land.

The wind has dissipated; the road seems better surfaced; mining is a recent dreamscape. The earth has not quite woken up to spring yet; dormancy lasts all but the 80 days available for the growing season. Still, the landscape exudes an awakening exhilaration. Proserpine crawls out from under the rocks. John Alla told me that miners are underground creatures of night. Diurnal cattle ranchers inhabit the sunny-side-up of the same earth.

Norm Glaser presents the vision of the cowboy rancher—tall, lean, muscled, wind-leathered skin over sculpted cheekbones, devastatingly handsome even at 73 years old—but lacks the cowboy drawl. He is one of the most intelligent and speedily articulate people I have ever interviewed. My hand scratches madly across my notepad, chasing his thoughts and experiences. So much for Westerns and Roy Rogers.

Ranching flows three generations deep through his blood, he tells me. "My grandfather was on his way to California to the gold mines in 1852. He worked as a freighter, teamster, and on ranches in California and remembered camping at the confluence of the North Fork and Humboldt Rivers. He thought of the valley panorama and the view to the Rubies. So he bought a herd of Durham cattle in Oregon and drove over Applegate Pass. He homesteaded in 1869 and was first on the tax roll in 1871." According to Norm, mining and livestock grazing have supported his family and the Nevadan economy since the 1860s. Lewis Rice Bradley, a successful cattle rancher, became state governor in 1870 and built a political infrastructure supporting ranching that lasted for decades, until 1933.

"At that time," Norm intoned gloomily, "a cowboy from Winnemucca named Phil Tobin, who was a senator—and he never lived to see Las Vegas—introduced a bill to legalize gambling. Actually, it was only legalizing what was already going on in the back rooms. If I had my choice in the legislature, I would have said we have a bear by the tail." Unlike other Elko residents, Norm views gambling skeptically, seeing it as a cause of juvenile delinquency and crime. Unlike mining and grazing, which are based on the land and "historically good," gambling, he insists, is uncertain. Reliable work comes with the solid earth.

The cowboy resurfaces as Norm recounts stories of looking for water, sleeping with snakes, and traveling with wagon trains. I smell campfires, hear "Home on the Range." Three generations of his family have ranched, camped and raised cattle together; the herd now numbers around 2,200 head of cattle, with about 1,000 new calves branded each year. Although he employs airplanes and four-wheelers for some scouting, Norm insists that "there's no substitute for horses. We've been ranching traditionally here for a hundred years. The government does everything but leave us alone. My brother and son, who ranch with me, and I are all conservationists with degrees in agricultural engineering, animal husbandry and veterinary science. We create retention ponds and duck ponds wherever we can. We have won numerous awards for conservation. We have a stable and static operation. We're limited by the amount of hay, land and water that's available. The government hassles us even more with permits, grazing fees and the like. Their object is to get rid of sheep and cattle men. Ranching is dependent on grass, which is a renewable resource, whereas minerals are finite. Agriculture generates about $500 million of wealth every year."

As there is so little rainfall for farming, Norm reasons that grazing constitutes a logical land use. He cites the historical respect that the government had for Nevada-controlled grazing, which reversed with the advent of environmental movements and the worries over endangered species. Whereas once Nevada owned most of its land, now the government owns roughly 90 percent of state land, rendering a very slender state tax base and depleted economy. A former state senator, Norman waged a legal battle with the federal government over ownership by initiating the Sagebrush Rebellion. "According to the Constitution, all states come into the Union on equal footing," he rages. "Well, it didn't work out that way. When Texas came in, the government didn't lay claim to one acre of land." While still pending a ruling by the Supreme Court at the time of the interview, Norm was confident that his Sagebrush Rebellion would remedy all that.

If cattle ranching is imperiled, sheep grazing suffers a still more precarious future, in Norm's view. Sheep have dwindled from roughly 1 million to one-tenth that number. Although sheep, who munch forbs, herbs and broadleaf plants, and graze symbiotically on the same land with cattle, who eat tall grasses, they compete less well with the wolves and coyotes that are "re-introduced" by the Fish and Wildlife Service. Norm scoffs at the research carried out by Stanford biodiversity scientists. "They already know the conclusions that they want. Scientific mockery: Just tell me what you want, and I'll develop the facts." Still, he smiles as he invites me to tour his ranch on my next trip to Elko.

As I leave Halleck, the late March afternoon darkens toward an early sunset. The sun no longer illuminates the mountains. Clouds shroud the mountains and cast dark shadows on the Humboldt. The plateaus stretch, vast and empty. From the bridge, I see little but stars and partnering water sparkles.

Back in Elko, I learn that sheepherding here dates back as far as cattle ranching. Protected by Governor Bradley's policies, ranchers built small, stable operations. As sheep often seek grass all year, smaller operations insure a flexible survival for both sheep and herder. As I learned at the chamber of commerce, many early sheepherders were Basques who had herded in the Pyrenees before fleeing Franco's regime. Knowing this bit of history eases my jaw-drop at finding Basques in what seems to be the least likely of places. The genius loci in Elko laughs easily, producing odd moments of surprise and ethnic diversity, while remaining friendly—like the people.

Basque names are prominent in local lore. Pedro Altube was regarded as the "father of Basques in America." Hot-tempered multimillionaire Pete Itcaina, another Basque sheepherder, waited seconds too long for a drink in the Silver Dollar Club. He bought the saloon and fired the bartender. For years, the Basques herded traditionally, using covered wagons, docking lambs' tails to obtain a count, and castrating lambs with their teeth. Then the number of Basque families willing to herd sheep dropped as federal regulations proliferated and permit prices rose. Most Basques now run stores or restaurants.

A first-generation Basque, Anita Franzoia owns Elko General Merchandising. As we talk, nimble-footed Anita simultaneously directs an employee, straightens bolts of cloth, and throws darting looks and smiles to customers who come and go. No wonder the Basques are so skilled at keeping track of mischievous flocks of sheep cavorting on high plateaus, I think, knowing the problems I have tracking two daughters. Although she speaks Basque and has been president of the club that sponsors the National Basque Festival, Anita tells me that few people use the language in Elko today. "At least my kids speak and understand it," she says and smiles. For years, her family owned stores and supplied the herders. However, "There's not many sheepherders left. There's some in Utah, some in Austin. The economy is bad for them."

Now, the largest sheep ranch lies near Tuscarora, owned by DeLloyd and Connie Sattherthwaite. Even before coming to Elko, I had known of Connie, who is president of the Woolgrowers Association. Actively working with environmentalists, Connie constantly reassures the government of the low impact of traditional methods on the land. She emphasizes the obvious omnipresent uses of wool and donates generously—quilts, blankets, wool, coats—to various charitable organizations. However, her battle remains that of Sisyphus, as environmentalists continue to introduce predators, and the government raises permit fees and seizes land.

Walking the streets of Elko, seeking the bridge for fresh air, I have an uneasy certainty of why the town has so many Basque restaurants. These people, too, need to eat.

Which Bridge?

> *You, moving down the road*
> *Must have a code*
> *That you can live by...*
> *Teach your children [parents] well...*
> —Crosby, Stills Nash and Young

Before I leave Elko, I return to the bridge. Avoiding the pavement, I approach on frozen earth, nubbled clods of mineral potential. The denuded bank slides into the river as I ascend the arch. Liquid bubbles and hums underfoot. My thoughts descant "People? Land? Water?" Back in Boulder, Colo., lines seem clearer cut. The city's tourist economy thrives on visitors who come downtown to shop after hiking in protected open space. In fact, fields, trees, mountains and their inhabitants regularly receive more tax support than the city's schools. Boulder's is an idealized, romantic ethic, privileging nature as Edenic open space. In Boulder, nature is the sublime wilderness. Here in Elko, nature is where Adam and Eve find themselves after being ejected from the garden. Here, nature is what one knows by the sweat of one's brow. Here, nature means work.

I feel unnerved by what I have seen. The blast at the mine was too literally mind-blowing and earth-shattering. The plateaus often seem bleak, overburdened. With a designer's eye, I see protected fields, reclaimed quarries filled with grasses, trees and uncontaminated water with paths alongside.

My other eye envisions John Alla, father and grandfather, drinking coffee with Buster. Norm Glaser reminds me that reliable work grows from the land. The fathers at Newmont shine golden with the knowledge that their children are receiving a high-quality education and will remain in town. Even Wendell Berry supports that. Anita Franzoia, Thelma, and Mary Korpi echo my feminist need to support my daughters with my talents.

Yet either eye's vision is as much a construct of work as the landscape I mentally redesign. Neither Elko as it is nor Elko "returned" to managed open space with introduced predators is the pristine wilderness lauded by outspoken environmentalists, a group with whom I have always associated myself. Until coming to Elko, that is, and meeting the people whose needs for survival are as real as those of the land and seemingly more tangible than those of legislators in Washington, D.C. However, I do not want to stand on a polemical bridge, whose opposing urban and open-space shores cannot withstand a political flood. Right now, Howe's "hunger that crosses the bridge" seems a human, devouring drive to dominate the land according to a single ethic, whether survivalist or environmentalist. Feeling that rapacious approach from either shore, I question a single vision, a bridging metaphor, to solve this standoff. I look for ways to connect the issues. Perhaps I seek the bridge of metonymy, touching parts that spiral into some larger whole.

Richard White offers one way of rethinking the political, human and landscape issues that pervade Elko. A historian, he locates the controversy in the perception of humanity as existing outside nature, which is "other" and conceptual. How one constructs "nature" reflects the way one personally experiences nature, physically and mentally. Whereas once that experience was in backbreaking labor, now it is usually in hiking, skiing and other forms of recreation. Describing the logging controversy over clear-cutting in Washington state, White cites the prevalent bumper sticker, "Are You an Environmentalist, or Do You Work For a Living?" According to White, we have shifted from a world that valued working physically with the land to one that holds itself apart from blue-collar labor such as mining and logging, which is seen as despoiling nature:

Most Americans celebrate nature as the world of original things. And nature may indeed be the world we have not made—the world of plants, animals, trees, and mountains—but the boundaries between this world of nature and the world of artifice are not very clear. Are the cows and crops we breed, the fields we cultivate, the genes we splice natural or unnatural? Are they nature or artifice? We seek the purity of our absence, but everywhere we find our own fingerprints. It is ultimately our own bodies and our labor that blur the boundaries between the artificial and the natural. …We cannot come to terms with nature without coming to terms with our own work, our own bodies, our own bodily labor.

According to White, environmentalists refuse to acknowledge the blurred boundaries, and they construct a pristine nature only accessible for leisure. They say little about humans and work. White suggests focusing on exactly what environmentalists ignore—the knowing of nature through work—to create the dialectical spiral that will move the polarities beyond their static position. Even environmentalists and writers, he says, affect nature through work; they just may not see their effects. He describes the process of his own writing:

I cannot see my labor as separate from the mountains [outside his office window], and I know that my labor is not truly disembodied. … The lights on this screen need electricity, and this particular electricity comes from dams on the Skagit or Columbia. These dams kill fish; they alter the rivers that come from the Rockies, Cascades, and Olympics. The electricity they produce depends on the great seasonal cycles of the planet: on falling snow, melting waters, flowing rivers. In the end, these electrical impulses will take tangible form on paper from trees. Nature, altered and changed, is in this room. But this is masked. I type. I kill nothing. I touch no living thing. I seem to alter nothing but the screen. …My separation is an illusion. What is disguised is that I—unlike loggers, farmers, fishers, or herders—do not have to face what I alter, and so I learn nothing from it.

White suggests that as long as we separate ourselves from nature and do not come to terms with our work, we will continue to create false dualities between nature and work. These are the kinds of dualities I have seen daily in Elko. Without realizing that we all work to survive within this landscape—miners, grazers, legislators and writers—and shape our land physically and mentally, we cannot evolve positively beyond the polemic. Thoreau was right. Soul and soil remain the defining dialectic of human survival.

The water stills into sunset. My reflection from the bridge is clear, multichromatic. In a few hours, I return to Boulder, to my children and my client's deadline. Most of my clients, excluding this one, seem to require endless upgrades of my computer to fit their technical and cyber needs, costing countless computer chips, endless energy. I rarely get things right the first time and write innumerable drafts on limited trees. I do not eat meat but let my children choose their own preferences. Fast-food hamburgers have crossed my linoleum-floored, Sheetrock-walled threshold. I recognize my footprints on the earth leading to the bridge. I wonder how I will get to the other side.

With White, I believe that no simple or stark choices provide paths to stopping environmental havoc. One set of footprints or fingerprints is not better than others. Pointing fingers does not do it. Three fingers will always point back to ourselves.

Now the arch proves a metaphoric bridge, an unbiased position where those who walk on the land and those who work with it unite in caring for that gift and for each other. That is, if we really *care* beyond rhetoric. Parenting has taught me that only by caring can we become accountable. I clutch the familiar metallic bridge rail. I look from land to town to mountains and then sink my gaze into the water. My face and the universe look back pensively. For the sake of the land and my daughters, I hope fervently that sooner rather than later we reflect on bridges and then relocate ourselves healthily in our landscapes.

Sarah Massey-Warren is a writer and landscape architect who lives with her daughters in Boulder, Colo. Her work has appeared in numerous magazines and journals, including Architecture, Cream City Review and Sniper Logic. She teaches writing at the University of Colorado-Boulder.

Father

Aine Greaney

*M*y father has fallen asleep by Athenry, the first stop out of the Galway station. His head is back against the seat, false teeth like a horse, his familiar smell of diesel and damp leather. I sit opposite, sipping coffee from a paper cup. Tea is far too country, and this, like the book I've taken from my shoulder bag, is to set myself apart, to hope that people don't guess that we're together—father and daughter. I'm going off to college in Dublin—a teacher-training college run by the Sisters of Mercy, recently gone co-ed but where first-year students live in the residence hall with a curfew of midnight on weeknights, 2 a.m. on weekends.

For this trip, he's dressed in one of his newer uniforms—navy-blue jacket and pants, silver buttons, blue shirt, peaked cap with its badge, and navy-blue tie with the letters CIE embroidered in yellow.

For over 40 years, my father drove a freight truck for CIE (Coras Iompar Eireann), the national Irish transport company. In our village and parish, fathers were mostly farmers. They farmed their fathers' and grandfathers' small farms with the unrushed pace of roadside talk from tractor to tractor or over the handlebars of their big, men's bicycles. It was unusual to work elsewhere, and though we saw no household evidence of the extra money or luxuries, my father's truck-driving job would forever make our family and our lives different. The roar of his battered car as it left the yard each morning, two, three hours before our neighbors even thought of stirring, was enough in itself to set us apart as something not quite nameable. Industrious? Greedy? Above ourselves?

His life was that job. He worked the longest hours of any man I've ever seen in any country, and to this day, he'll begin stories with,

"In my job now…" The stories are detailed accounts of treacherous truck journeys through sudden snow, or a shopkeeper in a town who slighted him, or a waitress in a café who always brought him extra potatoes on his plate.

His was a life of clocking in and clocking out, of setting the round, green alarm clock by the kitchen wall clock, and of tearing the 26 miles from our country village to the truck depot in the city in his cheap, rusting cars. "I wouldn't please them I'd be late," he would say, with that Irish mixture of reverence and grudging hostility for authority—for the "thems" of the world.

One job perk was discounted train travel—a number of free train trips each year, half off the rest of the time, even half off the boat to England and throughout the British Rail system. The English trips, of course, were never used, and the Dublin ones only for days like this or a summer trip with my mother when I interviewed for this college or when my older brother graduated from his own Dublin college.

The morning train keeps belting across the bogs and the country-side toward the middle of the country, stopping at country stations for women in head scarves, pale men who look as if they're bound for a Dublin hospital, young workers with suitcases after the weekend down home. By now, the peak of his uniform cap is wedged tightly between the seat and the train window, his snores getting louder, and from my book, I steal looks around the carriage, almost hoping for the looks of annoyance or derision that would confirm my teen-age conviction that everyone, everywhere, was somehow smarter than we were, jollier, more able to take the train to Dublin with purpose and wakefulness.

Once he drops me off at the college on the south side of Dublin, he'll take the train back down west again, back in time to work a full day, just with a later start. He has asked for this special favor, a shorter lorry drive today, no doubt telling "them," in a tone proud, defensive and apologetic, about the daughter going off to college. When this train pulls back into the Galway station, he'll drive another lorry to another town 50, 60, 100 miles away, return to the depot later than usual, and then drive home to the village where he will tell my mother that everything went grand. Not a hitch going up or down. Great day's work afterward. Daughter delivered to college.

It's the third of October, an unusually bright day, and I've been 17 for three days now. In the hot carriage, my wool-blend skirt itches and makes me sweat and shift in my seat, but I'm careful not to waken him, for anything would be better than the slow, protracted talk between a father and his second-youngest daughter.

In a rare bout of spending, my mother sent me last week to buy shoes and a skirt, saying that first impressions last, not to be going up there to the college in those gibbles of jeans; it's all very fine to wear them once I'm there a while, but you can never undo first appearances.

For the five years of secondary school, I have worn my bookish, studious image valiantly because, though I never admitted it, I believed I had nothing else to wear, no ticket to the giggling, sexually tinged talk of girls in a convent school. Better to bow out, to snootily set myself apart rather than beg, try for inclusion.

In the summer between school and college, and in the summers before that, I've read all of Walter Macken, A. J. Cronin, James Herriott, Taylor Caldwell, library books, books borrowed from my best friend, and on the train now, I'm reading a huge, paperback edition of Agatha Christie's biography.

In that summer I also trained myself to think in French, so that when I pedaled my bike the 3 miles to our nearest town, I would narrate my journey in French—the pendulous, melancholy green of the roadside, the houses we knew so well, the hill where I had to get off and walk the bicycle, the cow-dung-spattered tractors that rattled past.

In that last year of school uniforms and study for final exams, I envisioned myself at the big university in Galway, where my older sister and brother went, living in wild, student flats and returning home with the secrets and sex of their lives pulsing behind their now cool, jaded faces. Once there, I would still be studious, perhaps, but finally social, titillating, joining the English and French societies for wine-and-cheese parties, staying out all night, drinking, and being kissed by boys with long hair and sensitive faces. But now, those plans have changed, and I am headed to a teacher-training college.

When the train starts to pull in through the western suburbs of Dublin, he sits up, awake finally, eyes glazed. "Oh, I had a great sleep," he says, as he always says when he wakes up on the couch at home, as if sleep is a sumptuous treat. I'm still pretending to read the life of Agatha Christie.

He watches the straggle of gardens, terraced houses, discolored red brick, the lines of washing that hang limp and sodden in the morning chill.

When the train creeps into Houston station, he sits up fully, alert and proud. A railway station is where he clocks in and clocks out, where he's a real man, and even here, across the country in Dublin, he knows it; he knows the oil and the diesel and the dull orange of the freight containers that sit waiting for lorries and men like him, in uniforms like his, to drive them off through the morning to towns that he has been to.

On the footpath outside the station, I get my first smell of Dublin, a brewery smell like old coffee, acrid and warm enough so that years later, when as a tourist I take the airport bus into the bustling Celtic Tiger Dublin, it will be this smell I look for.

The double-decker bus comes, and the Dublin conductor is already impatient with this queue of country people with their suitcases and questions: "Will this bus bring me to O'Connell Bridge?" "Do you know where the Eye and Ear Hospital is?" "Does this bus go past Fitzwilliam Square?"

We have reached the top step, my father ahead and me behind on the next step below. He cocks his head, the peak of his uniform cap, at the young Dubliner as if to say, "Look, I'm one of you." The conductor stares at him, waiting for questions or money.

"I'm with the Galway Road Freight," he says conspiratorially, stubbornly oblivious to the queue of men and women behind us.

"Whaa—?" the conductor says rattily.

"I'm with the Galway Road Freight," my father persists, and this time he jabs a finger over his shoulder toward me and tells this young city conductor about "the daughter here going to college." Impatiently, the conductor waves us on and looks to the next passenger for fares.

Victorious, my father chooses the second seat from the back. With my well-stuffed, green rucksack on my lap, I jam myself into the seat, but he stands, boots planted apart on the floor, grabbing the back rail of our bus seat and leaning in over me to look out the window, as if sitting is only for paying passengers—plain-clothes civilians who don't know any better.

The bus rattles up Victoria Quay by the River Liffey. The sun is shining; the city is still coming awake—buses, bread vans, lorries on the quays, small groups of men and women in anoraks and coats huddled at bus stops, lunch bags and handbags under their oxters, billows of cigarette smoke in the morning air. When we pass St. James' Gate, my father, as I know he will, points out the Guinness brewery and tells me how many's the morning, even before it was light out, he drove a lorry-load of barrels out through that very gate.

The bus roars on, stops in traffic, only to start again, and my father keeps watching the street, the bus, the back of the bus driver's head. After one sudden stop and start, he grins smugly, eyes the driver's back, and says loudly, "I can't bear that fella's method of driving."

Since leaving the train, I have been waiting like a whipped cat for his every word, his too-happy oblivion, his assumption that we are just like anybody else, that there's nothing wrong with two country people on a bus finagling for free fares.

In the summer when my mother brought me up here for the college interviews, we took a taxi from the station that whisked us through back streets and shortcuts to the college and back again for the evening train. But my father has no doubts about finding his way in the city, no fear of buses and directions. After this, I know we take another bus out to the south side and that it will all take longer than the taxi. But how long? Two hours? One? An hour and a half at the most—before we're there, before he's gone, before I'm alone, wearing old, hand-me-down Levi's and facing a new life in the city. In my wool-blend skirt, I cringe and wait and count time.

The autumn sun blasts through the bus window. I stare out at the shops, the pubs with the red and black trim, names above the door like something from the O'Casey plays I've seen on television. Across the river the Four Courts, more pubs, news agent, sweet shop, and on the corner, a huge florist.

When our bus stops, our conductor points us to Eden Quay on the other side of O'Connell Bridge to wait for an old, black-and-cream double-decker, the 6A, which will take us not just out to Blackrock but all the way up Carysfort Avenue, where there's even a stop right outside the college. Can't miss it. The conductor bawls his directions above the idling bus. My father, who is already growing deaf, nods along at first but then shamelessly asks him to repeat it all. I am standing on the footpath, waiting with my rucksack, numb.

"Oh, aye," my father eventually bawls back at him, coming down the bus steps.

Before we head off across the bridge, he turns to give driver and conductor one last salute, something between a wave and thumbs up. "Okey-doke," he screams back through the bus door in a final farewell.

The No. 6A is a driver-only bus, meaning no conductor, and when the driver glances at my father's cap, he instantly reaches past us for the fare from the next passenger. In this bus my father sits down. Passengers get on and off, and we both grow silent, watching the passing houses and trees—Trinity College; Merrion Square with its Georgian houses; the Ringsend chimneys against the sky; Ballsbridge, where the horse show is; Sandymount, then Booterstown and finally a flash of the sea and a park before the bus swings down through the village of Blackrock.

When it turns up Carysfort Avenue, we are the only passengers left. We pass a house where James Joyce once lived, more houses with curtained windows, the lounge bar where my mother and I ate lunch after my interview and I changed out of my high heels and suit.

I cried bitterly the day I got the acceptance letter for this teacher-training college. But by the time I sent back the confirmation, I had consoled myself, wiped away the tears and set about something between resignation and self-persuasion.

The journey before this journey—the application forms the previous spring, the summertime interviews, the letter of acceptance that made my mother whoop in uncustomary joy—is, in a way, a story of youthful defeat. It is also proof that even 16-year-olds know their own, deep hearts. On this day and on the days before this, I know I do not want to go to this college, do not want to be a primary school teacher.

Now I know the battle to get me here was not a battle at all. It was a mother's victory long set, one that started on that day the previous spring when she—casually, so I wouldn't rear up or balk—persuaded me to fill out the applications at least and deliver them back to the career-guidance nun, no commitment, just to humor a mother. On that morning, she followed me out the door to the school bus to sprinkle my school bag, where the completed forms were, with holy water. Half laughing, I brushed it off, but laughing even more and with uncustomary coyness, she sprinkled again.

One concession becomes another and then another, until the intolerable becomes acceptable, so that when we cave in, we have told ourselves that we are only caving in to that last request, not the whole shebang. On that day on the bus I have been persuaded, too timid, too dreamy to dig my heels in, and best or worst of all, I have persuaded myself.

On this October day, I do not know that I will prove myself right, and that in the years that follow, teaching Irish children in a small, Midlands village will be a long winter of sadness. I do not know that by my early 20s, I will be counting time, my life, in terms of months, weeks, weekends, entire school terms, years—until it has all become a frightened desperation of a young heart. Knowing things—at least enough to stop them clicking fiercely onward—takes either courage or wisdom or both. At 17, I have neither.

The bus sags to a stop outside the college, and when my father inquires for the next bus back to the city, the driver tells him that he turns at the top of the avenue, only about five minutes, and if my father wants to wait, he'll collect him on the way back down.

He "okey-dokes" this one, too.

We stand together outside the gates of the college, my father with the straps of my green rucksack slung over his arm like a handbag.

"Sure, there's point in me going up there with you," he says, nodding toward the beautiful, red-brick campus in the trees.

"No," I say.

"God bless you so." He goes to hand over the rucksack. For a minute, it sits on the footpath between us. When he hugs me, I get the diesel and leather smell again.

I watch him hurrying down the footpath to wait for his bus outside the high walls of the college. He doesn't look back.

I hoist the rucksack on my back and walk up the long driveway, moving in and out of patches of shade under the copper beech trees.

On the day of the college interview, my mother and I walked together up this avenue, and she told me how she had once been here 17 years before, when she had come to visit my aunt, her youngest sister, who was here to train as a novitiate nun. She was pregnant with me then, and now here we were on this summer's day, me teetering along in high heels and a borrowed interview suit, she edgy and tired from trains, taxis and a rare trip to the city.

In another story, another family, this would be reason enough for a motherly resolve to enroll me here—a tidy resolution of the past, fulfillment of some pre-birth promise—roll up the film credits, lights up, and say what a lovely story. But it is our story and our family, so the plot is far thicker, denser than this, perhaps too thick to fathom or tell.

In the big, carpeted lobby with its glass display cases and the heavy brown doors and corridors that lead off to classrooms and lecture halls, there are lines of girls about my age or older, all in jeans and normal clothes, I notice, and yes, there are boys, though just a few. Each student is flanked by a mother in her best suit and a father who tends to check books and suitcases.

I can register myself, hand over the check they have written last night for a half-year's tuition; the other half they'll pay after Christmas. But first I choose the queue where they are handing out keys for our rooms in the residence hall. Hot in my hand is the piece of paper I got in the post after my acceptance. I have been assigned Room 40, and standing there, my skirt and winter shoes hotter and itchier than ever now, I recite the words in readiness for the girl at the glass window—name, room number, birth date if needed, until it's my turn and the girl hands me the first ever door key I've ever owned in my life.

Over in the old residence hall behind the college, where everything smells of furniture polish and waxed floors, I climb the stairs to find Room 40, turn the key in the door, throw down my rucksack on the single bed with the crimson, satin bedspread. I shed the wool skirt and get into my faded, patched Levi's and a new red sweatshirt. In the mirror above the hand basin, I comb my hair, splash water on my face, and look at myself. I think I look all right now, not as country, groovy, and nobody will notice me when I go back over there to stand in other queues.

Outside the residence hall, a shiny black Mercedes is pulled right up to the front door. A man with a round, pink face in gray slacks and navy-blue blazer takes matching luggage from the boot. His daughter has short, dark hair and the same round, expectant face. She stands by, giving him directions with the suitcases.

Walking down the path through the trees to the college, I hear their singsong Cork accents on the warm, autumn air. She calls him Daddy.

In 20 years, this story has had different endings. Once, when I lived on a street between two colleges in upstate New York, I made myself stand and watch on a late summer day while minivans and station wagons delivered that year's new freshmen to town. Like a sadist peeping Tom, I stood on the hot footpath to gawk at mothers in their shorts, blouses, loafers and handbags. I studied each face, each family — fathers in golf shirts and chinos carrying stereo systems, computer monitors, easy-assemble bookshelves across the shiny green lawns; freshmen in Dead-head T-shirts, Birkenstocks and premature goatees, who seemed to dance and skip above the ground with edgy, laughing anticipation. And I made myself think of that other day, of a father stumping across a Dublin avenue for his bus like a uniformed Winnie the Pooh. Afterward, I walked home along an American avenue, musing about past and present, about differences of time, place and social class. Before turning the key in my American house, I found and trapped some words, a line to wrap up a story.

Once, for a St. Patrick's Day reading at a library, I finished this tale with a quote from Hugh Leonard, the Irish playwright and columnist, who wrote about his own father: "Love, turned upside down is love for all of that." The audience sighed and said *Lovely, wow, leave it to the Irish.* And I drove merrily home in a cocoon of self-congratulation.

Another ending was a long, ruminating treatise about grown-up families, blue-collar children who have been educated to a place forever beyond their parents where they can name-drop wine labels, independent films, holiday resorts.

But there is no real ending yet — nothing to conclude or fathom the story of a man, a life and a lorry or a youthful day on a train, a bus and a campus.

How to end things that are still playing on, reeling and cranking through the mind and the heart?

Aine Greaney is an Irish native living on Boston's North Shore. Her work has appeared in various Irish and U.S. literary journals. She has received four writing awards, and her first novel is under consideration at a Dublin publisher. She teaches creative writing part time.

Adventures in Celestial Navigation

Philip Gerard

N: Proving Yourself Wrong

You begin by pretending you know exactly where you are.

You begin with a fiction.

On a chart of the inshore ocean—or on a blank universal plotting sheet you've laid out with penciled straight lines that represent the curved reality of Earth (another fiction)—you mark your position, a dark point on blank water.

You call this your *DR* position—for *ded reckoning*. You draw a semicircle above the point, so that it looks like an astonished eye.

Ded reckoning has nothing to do with mortality—the *ded* comes from *deduced*, what you think you know based on history: the history of the boat you're sailing in. Where she (all ships are feminine, after Minerva, the Roman goddess of navigation)—where she was when you last knew for sure. How fast she has been moving since, and in what direction. You draw a line along your true course to reflect that projected path: five hours, say, at 6 knots equals 30 nautical miles of distance along that course line from your last known position. You don't know yet what the tidal set and the currents have done to her. Or leeway—her tendency to slide a little sideways as she moves forward. As we all do.

So this point 30 nautical miles along your true course from your last position is the place where you think you are now. This is what you believe, but not too hard. Up until this moment, it has been the basis for all your decisions regarding the voyage, yet you are utterly willing to abandon it now.

You open your navigator's toolkit, your magician's bag of tricks: star finder, hand-bearing compass, chronometer, parallel rules, dividers, triangular protractor, nautical almanac, sight reduction tables, pencil, stopwatch, and the queen of all navigation devices, the sextant.

And you set to work.

Before you do anything else, you must observe the sky—not casually, like an idle passenger or a romantic dreamer, but accurately and with precision. Unless you're shooting the sun—sighting on it with your sextant—in broad daylight, you must make your observation at dusk or dawn, in the crepuscular light of a day dying or being born —during what's called *civil* or *nautical* twilight, depending on how many degrees the sun lies below the horizon. You search the sky in a certain compass direction and at a certain altitude, looking for some specific heavenly body, such as the planet Venus or the star Hamal, and recognizing it when you see it. Or else you work the problem from the other end: shooting it and, by means of its compass bearing and altitude, figuring out later which body it was—noting the time, down to the exact second.

Seconds matter. In navigation, time means distance in all sorts of ways. Four seconds' error in recording time results in an east-west position error of a whole nautical mile.

You aim the sextant by peering through a telescopic eyepiece. The sextant does something very simple and very difficult: It measures the angle between the navigator's eye and the celestial body being observed. It does this by rotating a mirror mounted on what's called an *index arm* along a curved and calibrated semicircular frame called the *main arc* until the body being shot is reflected exactly into another mirror, level with the horizon, called the *horizon mirror*.

In simple terms, with the sextant, you create an optical illusion in your eyepiece: placing a star or planet or the sun exactly on the horizon—otherwise known as *bringing down the body*. You have to love the language—full of absolute metaphor. All the other calculations depend on this first one, so the sextant must be reliable, precise and accurate to a fine tolerance.

You have just augmented a convenient fiction with a precise optical illusion.

Then, through applied science, spherical trigonometry, simple arithmetic, the accumulated wisdom of master navigators long in their graves, a nautical almanac, sight reduction tables, and a little magic, you prove yourself wrong: You're not where you thought you were.

You prove your boat is actually someplace else—if you're a good navigator, not too far from where you thought you were. Half a dozen miles, perhaps. Enough to make a difference.

You prove.

In an age of endless equivocation, the denial of absolutes, the wholesale refusal to believe anything for sure, the new academics' stubborn contention that all facts are relative, that nothing can be known for sure, that history is mostly a matter of point of view, not incontrovertible fact, you prove yourself wrong.

And in proving yourself wrong, you prove something else: exactly where you are.

It is not a matter of opinion. It is not open for debate. It is not arguable or biased by gender or ethnicity or influenced by national regimes or political agendas. It is not personal: You either miss the reef or you hit it. You either find the sea buoy that marks the entrance to your harbor or you pass it by in the night. You make landfall or you don't.

That's the beauty of navigation: It is unequivocal.

To set out from one harbor and arrive safely at a chosen destination is its own proof of success. And it carries with it the right to be at the new place—the place you found, without road signs or fixed highways. Hardly anything on earth is as exhilarating as sailing into a new harbor at sunrise after a nighttime passage offshore across open water.

Not long ago, we sailed into Cape Lookout Bight, formed by a sandy crescent on the North Carolina coast, just as the sun rose purple behind the eastern mare's-tail cirrus and the water was studded with scores of floating humps—great loggerhead turtles come to mate in the protected waters under the lighthouse. We glided by them silently, and a few adopted our sloop as we anchored, and floated alongside us all day.

What is it like to sail on the ocean out of sight of land? That's the question most often asked by people who have never been out of sight of land, except perhaps in an airplane. One answer: Navigating on the ocean is just like driving your car—if all the road signs were taken down and Earth's surface were flooded to a depth of at least 1 foot so that all features and contours were invisible under a flat, glassy surface—or under a wind-whipped surface full of swells and breaking waves—with, of course, rivers and lakes and canyons remaining as deep as they are and all other obstacles—rocks, fences, tree stumps, ditches, railroad tracks and so on—remaining in place.

Finding the hidden roads, keeping from the submerged hazards, dodging tractor-trailers and trains and buses coming from all directions and passing you on all sides at varying speeds and with varying degrees of skill and caution and courtesy—without any headlights, if it is night —and using as your reference not easy-to-follow signage but the mathematics of plotting your course—*that* would be a like challenge.

Celestial navigators most often rely on the sun, and if they shoot stars or planets or the moon, they must do so in a narrow window of opportunity at dusk or dawn, when the bodies are visible but there is also enough ambient light to power the monocular lens of the sextant.

For the navigator, the world is a sphere with a diameter of 6,888 nautical miles. When you achieve a celestial fix on that sphere, gridded into degrees, minutes, and even tenths of minutes of latitude and longitude, you are fixed for that instant, the solution to a complex exercise in mathematics. You are the variable that has been solved for.

NE: Steering by the Stars

A common misconception is that the celestial navigator shoots a star or planet and plugs the sextant reading into a formula and *voilà!* A perfect fix. But it isn't quite so simple. What you find after shooting one body and working out the math is a line—what's called a *line of position*, or *LOP*. You know you are somewhere on this line. And to make matters more complicated, that line actually represents a small segment of a very large circle.

Remember, we're trafficking in fictions in order to approach reality.

Imagine you are sailing around in utter darkness looking for a little island with a lighthouse on it in the middle of the ocean. You have no compass—and thus no idea whether that island is north or south or east or west from you. Then you spot it. The chart tells you that the light is a hundred feet high.

You know—don't ask me how—that there's an easy way to calculate how far away you are from the light: First you take the square root of its height plus 14 percent. The square root of 100 is 10; 14

percent of 10 is 1.4. So the sum is 10 plus 1.4, or 11.4 miles. But wait—you also have to add your own height of eye—height above the water. Say that when you stand on deck, your eye is about 10 feet above the water. So the square root of 10 plus 14 percent is 3.6. Add that to 11.4 and you realize you should be able to see the lighthouse at a distance of 15 miles in clear weather.

But since you don't know which direction you are from the lighthouse, all you know is that you are somewhere on a circle with a radius of 15 miles, with the lighthouse at its center.

Now pretend that that lighthouse is a star and that a straight line runs from the star to the center of the Earth—an imaginary tower on which the starlight is mounted.

The point where that line pierces Earth's surface is the *geographical position*, or *GP*, of the star—the imaginary island on which the light is located. Only this light is very high, so high you must measure its height by determining its angle above you with a sextant—remember, that's what a sextant does—which will give you degrees, minutes and tenths of minute of arc. Arc translates into distance at a rate of 1 mile per minute of arc. Since there are 60 minutes of arc to the degree, the circle you would draw around the star's geographical position based on the angle of that body to you would be hundreds, maybe thousands, of miles in circumference.

For example, if you measure the star at 40 degrees of arc, then its geographical position is 40 times 60, or 2,400 miles away from you. That's the radius of the circle on which you are located, which must therefore have a circumference of over 15,000 miles (π times the diameter of 4,800 miles).

Hence you must reduce the scale of the problem—reduce the circle to a segment. Reduce thousands of miles to a few dozen. This is why it's called sight *reduction*. All the calculations and tables allow you to do just that. And remember the fiction that anchors all this: You began by pretending to know exactly where you are—your ded reckoning position. If where you think you are is at all close to where you really are, you have narrowed the large circle to a small segment.

In any case, once you have two sights calculated, you plot them as two lines that—if the bodies were separated by an angle greater than 30 degrees, and ideally greater than 60 degrees—should intersect. The point of intersection is your fix.

If you can shoot three stars or planets, even better: Now you have the classic triangle of a three-star fix, and you are inside that little triangle—a space about as big as a city block.

E: Celestial Baseball

So the celestial navigator fixes a position with reference to the stars, including our sun, and the planets; the location of the ship is reckoned in the context of moving but predictable bodies in the heavens. Those heavenly bodies have complex relationships with the ship's tiny point of location on Earth—the sun, moon, each planet and star is assigned a geographical position for every hour and second of every day of every month and year: the point at which it would, theoretically, splash down on the surface of the Earth on its gravitational plunge toward the center of the Earth.

There is no fudging.

It is exhilarating and humbling to fix your location under the stars—a totally accidental use for the firmament, yet so compellingly precise that the imagination begs for the hand of a Supreme Being to have created such a remarkable instrument of absolute context.

Even the term testifies to this: *celestial*, as in *residing in the heavens*.

It would be like emerging from the steaming jungle and discovering a perfectly formed fossil baseball diamond in the wilderness of prehistory, eons before *Homo sapiens* prowled the Earth and the game of baseball was invented—with the pitcher's mound exactly 60 feet, 6 inches away from home plate, the bases 90 feet apart, all the mathematical relationships true, waiting for the day millions of years in the future when mammals would evolve into prosimians and, at last, primates and humans, and a Civil War general would invent a baseball, a bat, and a book of rules to codify the mathematical and geometrical relationships into a dynamic and meaningful experience.

You'd have to wonder if that baseball diamond were placed there by design, and if so, by whom?

And if so, why?

Now look up at the night sky and imagine that discovery of order on a scale so vast even level-headed scientists cannot comprehend its scope.

The celestial navigator exists in perfect context with the universe—which is more than most of us can ever claim for even a brief instant in life.

SE: Errors and Imperfections

All the above, of course, assumes you have computed accurately and made no errors—a very big assumption. The odds are very good that your sextant reading is off by a hair. After all, you are sighting a distant object from the deck of a pitching boat and trying to mark the exact hour, minute and second of the sighting. You may have forgotten to correct for the two kinds of errors common to sextants, especially well-used ones.

You can misread the arc of the body—its angle above the Earth— off the sextant scale. You can mistime the sight, or neglect to corroborate it properly with Greenwich Mean Time—the universal clock located on the prime meridian, the 0 degree of longitude, in Greenwich, England. The tables by which you extrapolate your position require rounding off and then interpolation to correct for rounding off. You might forget whether you are dealing with true degrees or magnetic, or add a correction instead of subtracting it. You might make a simple mistake in arithmetic—forget you are adding degrees, which contain 60 parts, and do the math in base 10, as you normally would, and wind up in the middle of a continent.

If you have made such mistakes, you will find out, and usually quickly.

There are all sorts of ways to check your work.

One way is to turn on your GPS—Global Positioning System— and let the satellites judge your calculations. Until about the year 2000, the military deliberately introduced an error into the civilian GPS signal—to thwart terrorists and rogue nations possessing guided missiles—so it was accurate to only half a mile or so. And in the spirit of true American can-do, the Coast Guard spent millions of dollars every year broadcasting a correction. Now the signal is accurate to 12 meters —the length of a smallish racing yacht—but, of course, the Coast Guard is still broadcasting a correction, so that the corrected signal is accurate to 3 feet.

Three feet. The span of your arm. You can stand up, extend your arm straight out in front of you, spin slowly and touch your exact position.

Don't mind the technology—once, the sextant was the most modern gadget on the block—and any honest navigator will use every trick he can to find his way across the blank ocean.

Or you can work out all your sights and compare—you'll look at your plot and see one line that goes off on its own and doesn't intersect the others, and you cast it aside. Working out that sight, you just went a-glimmering. Gremlins got into the works. The Imp of the Perverse.

Or you can let your gut tell you. The great circumnavigator Joshua Slocum, the first man known to have circled the globe alone aboard a sailing ship, always maintained he could tell which ocean he was in and what latitude simply by the color, feel and taste of the water under his keel.

Even I can tell from the surface of the sea when we've moved beyond 20 miles off shore, lost the continental shelf, or sailed into the Gulf Stream. Such information, the sensory residue of experience, is stored in your body—in your ears and stomach and eyes and probably even your blood, the way your immune system remembers diseases and how to survive them. The roll of the boat feels different. The color of the water turns from Atlantic gray to tropical aquamarine. The wave shapes are different, playing a different tune against the cutwater, as is the way rain squalls form on the horizon.

Sometimes the navigator at sea just feels an odd sixth sense operating—something doesn't feel right. It's not logical; there's no science to the feeling—at least none we know of yet—but for thousands of years the great navigators trusted their intuition as much as their instruments, and contemporary sailors are no different. Whatever the instruments say, if it *feels* wrong, it probably *is* wrong.

Sailors who make solo passages across oceans must sleep from time to time, and they report time and again how they rely on intuition to wake them in the event of trouble. After weeks at sea, they become tuned to their natural context in a way that is scarcely possible on land. With no landmarks, no artificial noise or distraction, listening day after day to the soughing whisper of wind, the creak of rigging, the slap and chirrup of waves against the hull, they can recognize at once the slightest variation in pitch and timbre and tone. They acquire an intuitive, overwhelming sense of exactly where they are, like the Eskimo, who recognize the subtle and familiar variations in what to us would seem a blank expanse of snow and ice.

S: Divine Aspiration

Now, here's the glorious part, the part the Knights Templars might have understood: Celestial navigation is an exact science, but it is also an art.

That is to say, the math offers a perfect answer to your position, but you are unlikely ever to achieve perfection in your practice of it. You will, as you get better and better, approach perfection. There is an unequivocally exact right answer, but you can navigate a lifetime and never reach it. The best you can hope for is an approximately right answer, equally unequivocal, approaching perfection.

In celestial navigation, there is an element of aspiration to the divine.

A very accomplished navigator will be able to fix his position within a mile's range; an inexperienced navigator may be 5 miles off.

Once into a long voyage, a gifted navigator may place the vessel exactly where reality has her and be able to prove it.

SW: Magical Captains

In the great days of sail, the captain of a ship was a figure of awesome authority.

His word was absolute law, enforced by the petty officer's knout, the master-at-arms' lash and the hangman's noose. In the British navy, which ruled the oceans from the time of the first Spanish Armada until the turn of the 20th century, the crews were made up of the sweepings of the assizes and jails and taverns—landsmen—along with seamen impressed against their wills from the merchant ships of a dozen nations. The captain remained physically aloof from these crewmen and often nearly as aloof from his officers. When the captain emerged from his cabin onto the quarterdeck, all officers retreated from the windward side to allow him private space. Except on ship's business, they dared not speak to him unless spoken to. More often than not, he dined alone. The loneliness of command was more than a cliché—it was an essential social and psychological buffer: The captain might at any time order his men and his fellow officers into catastrophic battle in which a third or more would routinely be killed or mangled.

The contingent of royal marines aboard each of His or Her Majesty's vessels was there as much to guard the captain and his officers from their own crew as to fight the enemy, and one marine always guarded the captain's door with drawn sword.

Yet the crews rarely rose in mutiny—though on a ship-of-the-line, the main fleet battleship, they might number three or four hundred, including men shipped as replacements awaiting the inevitable deaths of scores of their shipmates, as against a dozen officers and 50 marines. For the captain was not only the legal dictator of their daily lives, their judge and jury when they committed infractions; he also held the magical power of the sextant.

Many officers could navigate, more or less, and the teen-age midshipmen—future lieutenants and, with luck, captains—were gathered every morning on deck for lessons in celestial trigonometry, passing around the sextant and working out their sights with chalk and slate. In later times, ships even had skilled navigators specifically assigned to them, as coastal pilots are today put aboard in shoal waters or harbors.

But the captain was the genius of navigation. A captain who could navigate well commanded the trust of his crew—even if they hated him. The captain held the real key to their destiny—whether they could find their way through storm, hazard and enemy fleets home to England.

C.S. Forester's fictional Captain Horatio Hornblower—a composite based partly on two real-life naval heroes, Lord Horatio Nelson and Lord Thomas Cochrane—performs heroic feats of navigation in nearly every adventure. In one book, he is commanded to sail from England to the west coast of Central America without coming within sight of any land or any other ships—using only sextant and compass and slate board.

Think about that—the faith, the arrogance, that requires.

With his food and water all but depleted, he makes landfall exactly where he plotted it, exactly on time. As did the real captains Cochrane and Nelson, time after time.

On a schooner or merchant ship, the captain might be the only man on board who knew the art and science of navigation. To lose the captain to illness or death or mutiny—or madness, an occupational hazard—was to lose their way, literally, on the vast, untracked oceans of the world.

Christopher Columbus' crew came close to mutiny on his first outbound voyage, not because he was flogging them—he didn't dare—but because they lost confidence that he knew where he was going.

So the tools of navigation, especially the chronometer and sextant, took on a magical quality and were treated with the reverent care usually reserved for sacred relics: secreted in a chest in the captain's cabin inside elaborately carved and inlaid hardwood boxes, protected from salt and sea and rough handling. Even today, if you buy even a moderately priced metal sextant, it will come in a hardwood box or a bulletproof valise.

Imagine the illiterate sailor with no education in astronomy or mathematics, little sense even of the world's geography since he had probably never seen a globe, sailing along for weeks at a time with no land in sight in any direction. It must have seemed magical indeed that a man could put his eye to a strange metal contraption, scribble some queer numerical formulae on a slate, draw lines on a piece of paper, then tack his ship toward an invisible harbor, arriving there exactly as predicted.

A man who could do that, a captain, must be partly divine.

W: M. Thibault and the Greenwich Hour Angle

All my life, I have wanted to know how to plot a course under the stars.

Since my earliest days of reading Robert Louis Stevenson and Jack London—who taught himself celestial navigation during a Pacific voyage—the sextant has carried a mysterious power. The trigonometry daunted me, though—the slide-rule calculations. Words like *azimuth* and *intercept* and *horizontal parallax* and *meridian passage*. I studied trig in high school, even studied calculus, but the principles eluded me. And other matters took precedence—I didn't own a sextant, didn't know anyone who owned one, did not intend to become a sea captain for my life's work.

And anyway, by the time I became a sailor, electronic navigation had made the sextant obsolete as a primary means of navigation. For years now I have gotten along fine with GPS, which relies on a grid of satellites to locate a boat's position. A unit that fits into your pocket can be had for about a hundred bucks. Entering a harbor in fog or in the dead of night, I can also plot the contours of the land, locate the channel markers, and steer clear of other vessels using radar—like the GPS, another fruit of the military-industrial complex. But as I took to sailing on the ocean, I felt something of a fraud. It was time to do the things I had always yearned to do. My wife, Kathleen, bought me a celestial navigation class for Christmas. I finally had an excuse to buy a sextant and promptly sent away for one from a navigation supply house, along with a star finder and a radio-controlled clock that automatically sets itself to the naval observatory clock in Fort Collins, Colo., and is accurate to the second. I already had parallel rules, dividers and a hand-bearing compass—staple tools of ded reckoning navigation. I bought a nautical almanac and sight reduction tables, as well as a pad of blank universal plotting sheets and work forms for keeping the math straight while working out sights on stars, planets and the sun.

Before I ever set foot in the classroom, I read the textbook twice, taking my time—taking months, in fact. Doing every problem twice. Doing the difficult problems again and again until I got them right. The focus, the need to slow down and concentrate, was good for me. Celestial navigation, even reduced to formulae that I could mimic, did not come easily. There was nothing intuitive about it. It was an initiation into mystery, and you arrived at the mystery by numbers.

I found myself making simple errors of arithmetic over and over again. Mistakenly subtracting degrees, which contain 60 minutes, as if they contained 100. Entering the tables through the wrong coordinate. Plotting sun sights that were off by 50 miles. I knew they were off by that much because when I took them, I was standing in the driveway of my own house.

I read a paragraph about determining the Local Hour Angle from the Greenwich Hour Angle of the heavenly body, and my eyes glazed over and I heard a buzz inside my head, so I read it again, and again, and after a while it began to work—the way repetition on those foreign language tapes in high school gradually resolved into basic sense.

M. Thibault va à l'épicerie.
Mister Thibault goes to the grocery store.

To obtain Local Hour Angle, in West longitude subtract the ded reckoning longitude from the Greenwich Hour Angle of the body. If your DR exceeds the GHA, place a minus sign before the difference and algebraically add 360° to the result.

Translation: Since we know—and the tables tell you—the longitude of the heavenly body, to find out your own true longitude, you need to compare your assumed longitude with it. You will compare the sextant reading you took at this assumed longitude to the one you should actually have obtained if you were in fact at that longitude, and you will find this number by entering the sight reduction tables with the Local Hour Angle, which expresses that comparison.

To pass the American Sailing Association's Celestial Navigation Certification exam, the student navigator must be able to do the following—among many other tasks:

• Convert longitude into time.

• Apply the corrections for index error, dip of the horizon, and total correction to convert sextant altitudes of the sun, stars, planets and moon to true altitudes.

• Determine the latitude at twilight by means of the polestar.

• Determine the approximate azimuths and altitudes of the navigational stars and planets at twilight.

• Calculate the time of meridian passage of the sun.

• Calculate and plot the lines of position obtained from several celestial bodies at twilight and thus fix the boat's position.

• Find the boat's position using a running fix of the sun—that is, two or more lines of position from sun shots taken at different times.

The test takes the form of a simulated voyage across the Pacific, so that every answer depends on the accuracy of the previous answer's calculations, which means you can't advance to the next question until you have answered the previous question correctly. Every error compounds the next.

A mathematically inclined student can complete the exam in three hours. It took me seven.

NW: Ships in the Night

Navigation isn't all about stars.

Most navigation is more worldly.

Sometimes navigation is basic.

You're sailing, say, up the east coast from Charleston, S.C., to Wilmington, N.C., broad reaching on a starboard tack, so the wind is more behind you than in front, and you're coming up on the sea lane for the harbor at Georgetown, maybe 40 miles offshore. It's a black night, full of rain squalls and choppy, breaking seas running 6 and 7 feet, with a wind that has increased steadily from a breezy 10 knots to almost 25—just under 30 miles per hour.

You started off in the fairway of Charleston Harbor in bright sunshine, flying a spinnaker—one of those big, multicolored balloon-shaped sails. Now conditions are more challenging and, since there are only two of you on board, you've shortened sail and you're sledding along under a triple-reefed main and a handkerchief jib, with the wind behind you and to the right. Off your starboard bow, you spy lights. Because the sky is suffused with water vapor, the lights twinkle, and the pitching and rolling of the boat—*heeled* at, say, 25 degrees—make it hard to sight on the lights with binoculars.

After a few minutes of hard watching, you make out three lights: on the left, a red light; on the right, not far from the red light, another red light over a white one.

Fishing trawler, you decide. A 50-foot boat crossing ahead. No problem.

With your handheld compass, you take a bearing. In which direction is it located, relative to your boat? Every two minutes, you take another. After 10 minutes, the bearing hasn't changed a single degree, and you recall the simplest maxim of navigation: *If the bearing of two approaching vessels doesn't change over time, they are going to collide.*

You try the binoculars again. The other vessel is closing, and this time you see not three lights but five. Two were obscured by the halos —what navigators call the *loom*—of the other lights. Now the vessel is showing the same red light on the left but *four* lights—not two— stacked vertically on the right: Red-white-red-white, in ascending order.

It is not a 50-foot trawler but an 800-foot container ship, and the reason it didn't look very long on first sighting is the result of an optical illusion: The ship is heading to cross your path at an acute angle, so you're seeing a foreshortened version of its hull.

You do some quick mental arithmetic. You are sailing along at 9 knots—a little more than 10 miles per hour. The container ship is doing over 20 knots. In less than three-quarters of a mile ahead— 1,320 yards—your courses will converge.

He will run you down—a vessel bearing down on you is always a "he," from long nautical usage.

Your vessel is 32.5 feet long and displaces about 5 tons. The container ship displaces 50,000 tons and is seven stories tall. If you do collide, chances are very good he will not even know it. You and your boat and your sleeping crew will, of course, disappear in a lather of sundering fiberglass and twisted aluminum spars and roiling water. Whatever his bow bulb doesn't crush will be atomized by his gargantuan propellers.

Distance equals time: You have about six minutes to get out of his way. On a sailboat, six minutes is an instant. Even if the container ship were to stop all engines at this exact moment, the great vessel could not stop in time to prevent it from crossing your path.

And that path is wide and fraught with hazard. Even if he misses you, the suction of a great vessel steaming along will draw your boat toward his hull. If you don't smash into him too hard, you will scrape along his hull and might be sucked into the vortex of his great thrashing propellers. Even if he passes 100 yards off, he will throw a wake at you that can roll you onto your beam ends.

You call down the companionway—once. All you have to say is, "Ship," and your crew, your buddy, turns out on deck at once from a sound sleep, dressed in foul-weather jacket over sleeping sweats. Your buddy is a good shipmate, which means that when you call down the companionway in the middle of the night, he does not question, does not hesitate, does not complain, but simply turns out on a cold, wet deck swiping the sleep from his eyes and already grabbing the right lines to do the ship some good.

You bring the boat hard up into the wind and go close-hauled—sailing as close to the wind as you possibly can. The boat leans over hard from the added pressure of wind on sails. A wave breaks over the bow; spume scuds over the cabin top and drenches you, and the ride gets suddenly rougher.

But the bearing changes, and it keeps changing, as the massive black hull of the container ship sweeps by off the port bow, close enough to hit with a slingshot. You can hear the great engines thrumming, hear the machine noise leaking out the open ports of her towering superstructure, see rows of buttery cabin lights.

On the VHF radio, in halting English, her captain hails Georgetown for a harbor pilot, repeatedly, and Georgetown doesn't answer. He's oblivious to you, as you suspected all along.

But it doesn't matter now. You're safe.

You just solved a very basic navigation problem. It is not a matter of opinion.

Her blunt stern moves off, piled three-high with containers; your sailboat shoulders across the big ship's wake; your crew disappears wordlessly into the black hole of the companionway and sleep, and you ease the sheets and resume course, waiting for the clouds to clear off and the polestar to come out and the other stars to blink on, one by one in a perfect map, until they're smeared across the firmament from water to water, and they dissolve into the orange loom of sunrise.

Philip Gerard is the author of six books, most recently "Writing a Book That Makes a Difference" (Story) and the novel "Desert Kill" (Morrow; in paper and electronic formats from Disc-Us Books). He teaches in the creative writing department at the University of North Carolina at Wilmington, where he lives with his wife, Kathleen Johnson, and sails his sloop, Suspense, while at work on a new book of creative nonfiction.

Between the Lines

Report From a College Classroom: After the Terror

"In a peaceful age I might have written ornate or merely descriptive books, and might have remained almost unaware of my political loyalties."

—George Orwell, 1947

In his classic 1936 essay, "Shooting an Elephant,"—a frequently anthologized essay in freshman composition textbooks—George Orwell, an Imperial Indian policeman in service to His Majesty's empire in 1920s Burma, is goaded by several thousand members of the Burmese populace into killing a testosterone-charged elephant that has been responsible for the death of a laborer.

Sighting the mammal in the crosshairs of his German rifle, Orwell pulls the trigger repeatedly, instigating the pachyderm's protracted demise, an apt metaphor for his perception of a British empire in its own death throes. For years, my composition students, who might ordinarily have balked at the prospect of studying British colonial politics, are captivated

by Orwell's vivid imagery, anchored by precise detail:

In that instant, in too short a time, one would have thought, even for the bullet to get there, a mysterious terrible change had come over the elephant. He neither stirred nor fell, but every line of his body had altered. He looked suddenly stricken, shrunken, immensely old, as though the frightful impact of the bullet had paralysed him without knocking him down.

In the aftermath of the terrorist acts of September 11, this passage haunts me. How like the stricken beast in Orwell's tale did we all seem, numbed by the fiery images of the World Trade Center and the Pentagon seared in our brains, images rendered indelible by their relentless television repetition and our compulsion to both watch them and recoil from them.

That week my students' own works in progress—(what Orwell might have called "merely descriptive" scenes) based on clips from popular films like "Cast Away" and "A River Runs Through It"—seemed somehow shrunken, their significance paled by the real-life onslaught. How would experienced practitioners of creative nonfiction, we wondered, write about this cataclysm?

To find out, we read Adam Gopnik's New Yorker essay, "The City and the Pillars" (Sept. 24, 2001). Since my students soon would be crafting essays based on their own immersions in fast-food joints and retirement homes, in libraries and bowling alleys, Gopnik becomes our newest role model, though we wish no such devastation upon ourselves. The author walks in his beloved city, immersing us in its usual rhythms, its new smells, its ashy smoke that lingers to "wreathe the empty streets." Then Gopnik travels back in time, relying on Edgar Allan Poe's quirky maritime fiction of 1838, "The Narrative of A. Gordon Pym," for its awesome rendering of an Antarctic scene eerily similar to that of a scarred 21st-century Manhattan. Poe had written:

"The white ashy material fell now continually around us," [Pym] records in his diary, "and in vast quantities. The range of vapor to the southward had arisen prodigiously in the horizon, and began to assume more distinctness of form. I can liken it to nothing but a limitless cataract, rolling silently into the sea from some immense and far-distant rampart in the heaven. The gigantic curtain ranged along the whole extent of the southern horizon. It emitted no sound."

Gopnik then comments, "Poe, whose house around here was torn down not long ago, is a realist now." Meanwhile, our nation's literary pundits—like ringside referees—declare fiction dead, truth stranger.

But how to make sense of the incomprehensible without sacrificing the artistic? Orwell had figured out quite early in his all-too-brief career that this was nonfiction's nobler mission. In his 1947 essay, "Why I Write," he recalled his own youthful admiration for one of creative nonfiction's chief building blocks: intimate detail. He took pleasure in composing with a "meticulous descriptive quality"— what he called "aesthetic enthusiasm." Yet as he matured, he criticized his purple-prose phase. His disillusionment with imperialism, with the tumultuous 1930s—he mentions Hitler and the Spanish Civil War— shaped his sense of nonfiction's broader motives: to seek an understanding of history, to affect political thinking in the world. Fusing the aesthetic with the historic and political, Orwell's "Shooting an Elephant" endures as moral commentary for every age, a reminder of humankind's persistent inhumanity.

In late September 2001, my students and their counterparts across the country are asking why the attacks on the World Trade Center and the Pentagon happened.

"Why did *they* do this to *us*?"

Hard question. But we are not a global politics class; I am no historian. I abandon, for a time, my careful array of sequential lessons that lead students from scene-writing exercises to dialogues, from immersions and fact-gathering to first drafts and polished manuscripts. Though we regularly examine model works (often "slicing" selections into blocks of type and rearranging them to appreciate their architecture), this extraordinary time seems to demand an extraordinary departure: We form circles and read aloud, seeking to ease the palpable, ever-present tension that resides below the surface of our days. Media commentators, with their shoot-from-the-hip speculations, do not wholly satisfy. We agree some stories bolster us. Even victims' obituaries in the New York Times, having undergone a stylistic metamorphosis, have become capsules of shattered joy.

For deeper insights, though, we must turn to creative nonfiction—to the best of the recent work we can find. Eventually, we will visit the world of a Palestinian martyr, Ahmed Abutayeh, and spend a week in Gaza. But first to Afghanistan. We sample William T. Vollmann's lengthy article, "Across the Divide," revived from the New Yorker archives (May 15, 2000) and posted online eight days after the terror:

Jalalabad, a city 40 miles west of the Khyber Pass, has a rural feel, with long strings of laden camels on the main streets and packed-earth dikes curving crazily through the wheat fields just outside town.

With Vollmann as our guide, we travel on "bomb-cratered" roads through the snowy streets of Kabul; to villages, homes and secret apartments, where the Koran is caressed, where tea is served, where stories of unspeakable brutality emerge, where women find someone who will listen. We meet a cross section of Afghan society—even members of the Taliban; many of the people are starving, widowed, orphaned, the long-suffering victims of terrors that dwarf our own national grief.

Several days later, after our reading circles have moved to other manuscripts, other realms, U.S. bombs strike many Afghan targets, among them Jalalabad, the place where our reading journey began. The moment is unprecedented for all of us. My students wonder about the survival of the people we met. They wonder how many others have read Vollmann's story. They wonder at the efficacy of political prose, wonder what Orwell would say. And they wonder at the irony—that words carried us there first, before our bombs came.

—*Rose Toubes*

The Princeton Anthology of Writing: Favorite Pieces by the Ferris/ McGraw Writers at Princeton University
John McPhee, Carol Rigolot, eds.   *Princeton Univ. Press, 2001, 376 pp*

Here are some facts about a 10-year-old boy in Chicago:

Of all the men in his family's life, Nicholas is perhaps the most dutiful. When the television picture goes out again, when the three-year-old scratches the four-year-old, when their mother, Angela, needs ground beef from the store or the bathroom cleaned or can't find her switch to whip him or the other children, it is Nicholas's name that rings out to fix whatever is wrong. He is nanny, referee, housekeeper, handyman. Some nights he is up past midnight, mopping the floors, putting the children to bed and washing their clothes in the bathtub.

And here is what life was like before the attack at Columbine High School:

High school is a haunted house in April, when seniors act up because they know the end is near. Even those who hate it sometimes cling to the devil they know. And for the kids who love it, the goodbyes are hard to think about. Two weeks ago, Sara Martin was chosen to be a graduation speaker for Columbine High, and she was struggling. She wanted to write about all the people she loved, in the choir and the Bible club and even the ones who turn left out of the right-hand lane in the parking lot.

Nicholas and Sara are characters. They are characters found and described by the New York Times' Isabel Wilkerson and Time's Nancy Gibbs, respectively—and they appear alongside each other and alongside dozens of other characters in "The Princeton Anthology of Writing," edited by Carol Rigolot and John McPhee. McPhee, besides writing for the New Yorker, is the Ferris Professor of Journalism at Princeton. Rigolot is on the Council of the Humanities at the school. And for some 25 years, McPhee has taught nonfiction writing to handpicked undergraduates. This anthology is a collection of writing by working journalists who have come to Princeton for a semester to tell students their thoughts about writing.

You don't have to read deeply between the lines of this book to realize that a central message in many of those Princeton classrooms, no matter who was taking attendance, was this: Facts rule. Further explained, facts are the basis on which nonfiction writers succeed or fail, on which a story rises to art or falls to mere gossip. The picture of the facts—how they are arranged, stacked up, spread out, aligned, segregated, whatever—is crucial. But so too is the collection of the facts, the reporting, the hanging out, the being there for the right moment that closes a story or opens it or moves it in a direction that causes someone lying on a couch and reading to suddenly sit up. It's a 10-year-old boy being a father, a nanny, an uncle all at once; a high school senior trying to plan a small part of her life right before it is changed forever.

For some perspective on how far such factual writing has come, one need only listen to the facts McPhee imparts in this introduction:

When I was an undergraduate at Princeton, one of my favorite professors was Willard Thorp. In the English Department, we did not study contemporary journalistic prose. In the conversation, nonfiction was not yet a term, let alone a literary term. Its synonyms were tainted by the fish they had wrapped. Even as late as 1973, a Harvard anthology purporting to represent all the important writing done in the United States since the Second World War did not include a single nonfiction example. As this book splendidly attests, factual writing has found its place in the regard of the academy, to the great pleasure of all of us who are represented here.

The following fact should come as no surprise:

Hundreds, if not thousands, of the students who sat in McPhee's and the guest teachers' classrooms have become professional writers. More than a handful have won Pulitzer Prizes, journalism's highest honor, its Academy Award. The anthology's table of contents presents quite a faculty: Jonathan Schell, Roger Mudd, Victor Navasky, David Remnick, Alice Steinbach, Nat Hentoff—and dozens of others whose names aren't as well-recognized but who are nonetheless talented.

But names alone do not make a teacher. Many young writers who have enrolled in graduate programs based solely on their faculty rosters have been disappointed. Most writers have probably heard a story or two on the matter. Perhaps one or two of the teachers represented in this Princeton anthology disappointed a young writer, as well, but in reading this book, it occurred to me that the cliché *Those who can't, teach* probably wouldn't be a fair summary for the book.

There is a lot to learn from this anthology.   —*Michael Rosenwald*

Michael Rosenwald *lives in Cambridge, Mass., and works as a reporter for the Boston Globe.*

Rose Toubes *teaches composition and journalism at Des Moines Area Community College, where she served as the student-newspaper adviser for over a decade. Prior to her teaching career, Toubes worked as a business journalist for an Iowa-based subsidiary of the Hearst Corporation. She holds a master's degree in mass communications from Drake University in Des Moines.*

Bread Loaf
Writers' Conference

August 14-25, 2002

Michael Collier, Director
Devon Jersild, Administrative Director

Faculty Include: David Bradley, Vikram Chandra, Robert Cohen, Michael Collier, Ted Conover, Toi Derricotte, Ursula Hegi, Kevin McIlvoy, Carol Muske-Dukes, Sigrid Nunez, Steve Orlen, Carl Phillips, Helen Schulman, Alan Shapiro, Jim Shepard, Tom Sleigh, Susan Straight, Terry Tempest Williams
Special Guests Include:
John Elder and Galway Kinnell

Application Deadline: April 20, 2002
Financial Aid Deadline: March 1, 2002

For information and application materials contact:
The Bread Loaf Writers' Conference
Middlebury College, Middlebury, VT 05753
E-mail: blwc@middlebury.edu
Telephone: 802-443-5286

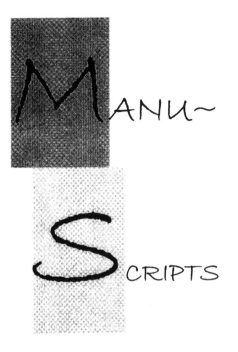

MANU~SCRIPTS

WANTED: LITERARY ESSAYS & MEMOIRS BY WRITERS WITH MULTIPLE SCLEROSIS

AND BY WRITERS WHO HAVE BEEN THE PARENT, CHILD, SPOUSE, FRIEND, AND/OR CAREGIVER OF A PERSON OR PEOPLE WITH MULTIPLE SCLEROSIS. LITERARY QUALITY THE PRIMARY CRITERION FOR INCLUSION IN OUR UPCOMING MS ANTHOLOGY. WILL CONSIDER SIMULTANEOUS SUBMISSIONS AND PREVIOUSLY PUBLISHED WORK IF NOTED AS SUCH. A PERCENTAGE OF THE PROCEEDS FROM SALES OF THE ANTHOLOGY WILL BE DONATED TO THE NATIONAL MULTIPLE SCLEROSIS SOCIETY. MAIL SUBMISSIONS TO:

TRACY EKSTRAND, EDITOR
MS ANTHOLOGY
P.O. BOX 272027
FT. COLLINS, CO 80527-2027

ENCLOSE #10 SASE OR E-MAIL ADDRESS FOR RESPONSE (MSS. WILL NOT BE RETURNED). QUESTIONS? E-MAIL tekst@juno.com OR CALL (970) 226-4884

The Body and the Book

Writing from a Mennonite Life

Essays and Poems by
JULIA KASDORF

This collection of essays by nationally known poet Julia Kasdorf "probe," in her own words, "the tangled threads of gender and cultural/religious identity as they relate to the emergence and exercise of literary authority." Her ten essays, accompanied by forty-two engaging illustrations (from a nude by Titian, to family photos, to a famous image of Marilyn Monroe) and a dozen of her poems, focus on specific aspects of Mennonite life. Often drawing from historical episodes or family stories, Kasdorf pursues themes of martyrdom, landscape, silence, the body, memory, community, and the struggle to articulate experience with a voice that is both authentic to the self and a conversation with her traditional Mennonite and Amish-Mennonite background.

$26.00 hardcover

"I read *The Body and the Book* in a few sittings and found myself eager to get back to it when I had to put it down. Each section speaks to the others through a graceful, articulate narration and inquiry. On Mennonite culture and identity, Julia Kasdorf has made a fascinating, honest quilt of stories and histories, questions and answers, bodies and books."
—Laurie Kutchins, author of *The Night Path: Poems*

The Johns Hopkins University Press
1-800-537-5487 • www.jhupbooks.com

Remembering Korea 1950
A Boy Soldier's Story
H. K. Shin

"*Remembering Korea 1950* is the story of a young boy caught in the throws of a terrible civil war, trying to survive while retaining a vestige of his humanity. H. K. Shin takes us inside the mind and experience of a young Korean soldier, and we come to see the war from the inside, undoubtedly as many Koreans saw it. This memoir offers a voice and perspective that are sorely lacking in the English-language literature on the Korean War."

—Carter J. Eckert, director of the Korea Institute at Harvard University

176 pages
paper $17.95

Personal and Provocative

Living in the Country Growing Weird
A Deep Rural Adventure
Dennis Parks

"A lot of young people headed for the hills in the '60s and '70s, but very few of us lasted. In this funny, funky, and wise memoir, internationally known potter Dennis Parks tells the rest of us what we have been missing all these years—from glorious mountain sunrises to the alarming post-coital hungers of female bunny rabbits."

—Harper Barnes, author of *Blue Monday*

152 pages, 22 b/w photos
paper $21.95

University of Nevada Press
toll free 1-877-NVBOOKS
www.nvbooks.nevada.edu